WRITERS AND THEIR

ISOBEL ARMSTRONG
General Editor

BRYAN LOUGHREY
Advisory Editor

Walter Pater

WALTER PATER

from a drawing of 1872 by SIMEON SOLOMON, *reproduced by courtesy*
of Fondazione H. P. Horne, Florence

Walter Pater

Laurel Brake

Northcote House

in association with
The British Council

© Copyright 1994 by Laurel Brake

First published in 1994 by Northcote House Publishers Ltd, Plymbridge House, Estover Road, Plymouth PL6 7PZ, United Kingdom. Tel: (0752) 735251. Fax: (0752) 695699.

British Library Cataloguing-in-Publication Data
A catalogue record for this book is available from the British Library

ISBN 0 7463 0716 0

Typeset by PDQ Typesetting, Stoke-on-Trent
Printed and bound in the United Kingdom by BPC Wheatons Ltd, Exeter

Contents

Biographical Outline

1839	4 August. Born in Shadwell, south-east London.
1842	28 January. Father died.
1845?	Family including his aunt Elizabeth and his grandmother moved to Enfield, north of London.
1848	Grandmother died in Enfield.
1853	February. Family moved to Harbledown, near Canterbury, Kent. Pater entered the King's School, Canterbury, as a day boy (member of the 'Triumvirate').
1854	February. Henry Dombrain entered the King's School (member of the 'Triumvirate').
	25 February. Mother died.
1855	February. John Rainier McQueen, son of the commander of the Canterbury depots during the Crimean War, entered the King's School (member of the 'Triumvirate').
1856	Pater wrote a number of poems including 'St Elizabeth of Hungary', 'The Chant of the Celestial Sailors', and 'Poets Old and New', later burnt.
1857	Poem, 'Cassandra'.
1857(–67)	Matthew Arnold elected Professor of Poetry at Oxford. Delivered lecture series throughout term of office, some of which Pater attended.
1858	5 August. Speech Day, King's. Pater awarded an Exhibition of £50, for three years.
	October. Sisters and aunt moved to Heidelberg. Pater entered Queen's College, Oxford. Tutor was W. W. Capes.
	December. In Heidelberg.
	Poems: 'Song of a Mermaid', 'My Cousin', 'The Acorn', 'The Fan of Fire'.

1860	Coached for Moderations by W. B. T. Jones.
	Summer vacation in Heidelberg.
	Poems: 'Greek Minstrel's Song', from 'Iphigenia', 'Oxford Life'.
1860–1	Wrote tutorial essays for Benjamin Jowett.
1862	Coached for final schools by Edward Boyle.
	11 December, BA Second Class Honours in Literae Humaniores.
	McQueen wrote to Bishop of London to object to Pater's alleged plan to become a priest. Pater remained in Oxford as private tutor while applying for Fellowships.
	28 December. Pater's aunt Bessie died. Pater travelled to Dresden and accompanied his sisters back to Britain.
1863	Took Charles L. Shadwell as a private pupil. Elected to Old Mortality Society with his friend Ingram Bywater. Competed unsuccessfully for clerical fellowships at Trinity College, Oxford, and Brasenose.
1864	February. Elected to first non-clerical fellowship at Brasenose as probationary Classical Fellow.
	February. Read essay, 'Subjective Immortality', to Old Mortality.
	July. Read essay 'Diaphaneitè', to Old Mortality.
1865	Summer. Visited Ravenna, Florence, and Pisa with Shadwell.
1865–6	August 1865–August 1866. Destroyed his poetry.
1866	January. Published 'Coleridge's Writings' (review), unsigned, in *Westminster Review*.
1867	January. Published 'Winckelmann' (review), unsigned, in *Westminster Review*.
	Became lecturer at Brasenose. Early lectures on the history of philosophy heard by T. H. Ward.
	Summer. With T. H. Ward at Sidmouth.
1868	October. Published 'Poems by William Morris' (review), unsigned, in *Westminster Review*.
1869	November. Published 'Notes on Leonardo da Vinci' in *Fortnightly Review*. First signed publication.
	Elected to New (later the Savile) Club.
	Took house at 2 Bradmore Road, in north Oxford, with his sisters.

1870(–79)   John Ruskin elected as first Slade Professor of Art at Oxford. Delivered lecture series throughout term of office.

          August. Published 'A Fragment on Sandro Botticelli', signed, in the *Fortnightly Review*.

1871   October. Published 'Pico della Mirandola', signed, in the *Fortnightly Review*.

          November. Published 'The Poetry of Michelangelo', signed, in the *Fortnightly Review*.

1872   July. Published review of *Children in Italian and English Design* by Sidney Colvin, in *The Academy*.

          Wrote 'Aucassin and Nicolette', 'Luca della Robbia', 'Joachim du Bellay', and 'Preface' for forthcoming book on the Renaissance.

1873   February. Published *Studies in the History of the Renaissance* with Macmillan.

          February. Pater visits the artist Rebecca Solomon, sister of Pater's good friend, the artist Simeon Solomon, at the time of Solomon's arrest and trial for gross indecency.

          November. W. W. Capes preaches sermon criticizing the new 'humanitarian culture' (of *Studies*).

          Louise Creighton and other women organize lectures and classes for women in Oxford which Clara Pater attends.

1874   21 February. Correspondence between Pater and W. M. Hardinge, an undergraduate at Balliol; Pater seen and privately castigated by B. Jowett, Master of Balliol. Hardinge 'sent down' for short period; Pater warned.

          25 February. Pater passed over in nomination for University Proctorship by Brasenose.

          April. Published 'On Wordsworth', signed, in the *Fortnightly Review*.

          November. 'Fragment on *Measure for Measure*', signed, in *Fortnightly Review*.

1875   September. Oscar Browning, Pater's friend, dismissed from his post as master at Eton.

1876   June–December. *The New Republic* by W. H. Mallock appears in serial form in *Belgravia*. Pater is satirized as Mr Rose.

November. Published 'Romanticism', signed, in *Macmillan's Magazine*.

29 November. Delivered lecture, 'Demeter and Persephone', at Birmingham and Midland Institute.

December. Published 'A Study of Dionysus', signed, in *Fortnightly Review*.

1877   January. Permitted his name to go forward as a candidate for the Professorship of Poetry at Oxford.

March. 'The Greek Spirit in Modern Literature' by Revd R. Tyrwhitt appeared in *Contemporary Review*; Tyrwhitt, rector of St Mary Magdalen, Oxford, attacked Arnold's Hellenism on the grounds of its atheism and J. A. Symonds's for its advocacy of homosexuality.

Pater withdrew his name as candidate for Professorship of Poetry.

24 May. Published second edition of *Studies*, retitled *The Renaissance: Studies in Art and Poetry*. 'Conclusion' omitted.

July. Ruskin attacked Whistler's art in *Fors Clavigera*. Whistler sued for libel.

Summer. Visited Normandy, Brittany, and the Loire.

October. Met Oscar Wilde, an undergraduate at Magdalen, Oxford.

October. Published 'The School of Giorgione', signed, in *Fortnightly Review*.

1878   April. Read essay, 'Love's Labours Lost', to New Shakespeare Society.

August. Published 'Imaginary Portraits 1. The Child in the House', signed (although Pater requested anonymity), in *Macmillan's Magazine*. The first published reference to 'imaginary portraits'.

October. Published 'The Character of the Humourist: Charles Lamb', signed, in *Fortnightly Review*.

25–6 November. *Ruskin* v. *Whistler* libel trial.

30 November. Cancelled publication of a projected volume with Macmillan titled *'Dionysus' and Other Studies* (initially *'The School of Giorgione' and Other Studies*).

1879   No publications.

Somerville Hall opened; Clara Pater a tutor in Classics.

1880   February. Published 'The Beginnings of Greek Sculp-
        ture. I. The Heroic Age of Greek Art', signed, in
        Fortnightly Review.
        March. Published 'The Beginnings of Greek Sculpture.
        II, The Age of Graven Images', signed, in *Fortnightly
        Review*.
        April. Published 'The Marbles of Aegina', signed, in
        Fortnightly Review'.
        Published 'Samuel Taylor Coleridge', in *The English
        Poets: Selections*, vol. iv, edited by T. H. Ward and
        published by Macmillan.
        Spring. *Boy Worship*, an anonymous pamphlet, ap-
        peared. C. E Hutchinson, its author, at Brasenose,
        1873ff.
        September. 'The New Renaissance' by H. Quilter
        appeared in *Macmillan's Magazine*. Its attack on
        aestheticism contested by W. M. Rossetti in December.
1881   No publications (working on *Marius*).
        Pater met 'Vernon Lee' (Violet Paget), who became a
        close friend of Pater and his sisters.
1882   No publications (working on *Marius*).
        December. Visited Rome re *Marius*.
1883   7 March. Published anonymous review of an anony-
        mous book of poems, *Love in Idleness*, in Oxford
        Magazine.
        Published 'Dante Gabriel Rossetti', in *The English
        Poets*, ed T. H. Ward, vol iv, second edition.
        Resigned tutorship at Brasenose.
1884   No publications.
1885   Served as Curator of the University Galleries, Oxford.
        25 February. Published signed review of *The English
        School of Painting* in *Oxford Magazine*.
        4 March. Published *Marius the Epicurean*, Macmillan.
        October. Published 'A Prince of Court Painters', signed,
        in *Macmillan's Magazine*.
        July. Candidate for Slade Professorship of Fine Art at
        Oxford. Unsuccessful.
        August. Relinquished Bradmore Road house in Oxford,
        and rented house with sisters in London, 12 Earl's
        Terrace, Kensington.

Met George Moore.

12 November. Second edition of *Marius* issued.

1886 17 February. Published anonymous review, 'Four Books for Students of English Literature'; first of series of unsigned reviews by Pater in the *Guardian*, an Anglican weekly newspaper.

March. Published 'Sebastian van Storck', signed, in *Macmillan's Magazine*.

17 March. Published anonymous review of *Amiel's Journal* in the *Guardian*. The book was published by Macmillan and translated by his friend Mrs Humphry Ward.

May. Published 'Sir Thomas Browne', signed, in *Macmillan's Magazine*.

October. Published 'Denys L'Auxerrois', signed, in *Macmillan's Magazine*.

November. F. W. Bussell elected as probationary clerical Fellow at Brasenose.

27 November. Published 'English at the Universities', signed, in the *Pall Mall Gazette*, a daily newspaper.

December. Published signed review of *La Morte* by M. Feuillet in *Macmillan's Magazine*.

1887 Clara Pater became Resident Tutor at Somerville.

24 April. Pater's older brother, William, died.

May. Published 'Duke Carl of Rosenmold', signed, in *Macmillan's Magazine*.

24 May. Published *Imaginary Portraits*, Macmillan.

5 August. Published anonymous review of *Juvenilia* by Vernon Lee (friend) in *Pall Mall Gazette*.

November. Published anonymous review *Serenus, and Other Tales* by M. Lemaitre in *Macmillan's Magazine*.

9 November. Published anonymous review of *An Introduction to the Study of Browning* by Arthur Symons (friend) in the *Guardian*.

1888 January. Third edition of *The Renaissance* issued; amended 'Conclusion' restored.

Matthew Arnold died.

28 March. Published anonymous review of *Robert Elsmere* by Mrs Humphry Ward (friend) in the *Guardian*.

June–October. Published *Gaston de Latour*, signed, in

five parts in *Macmillan's Magazine*. The novel remained unfinished.

27 June. Published anonymous review, 'Their Majesties' Servants', in the *Guardian*.

7 August. Pater met Arthur Symons.

25 August. Published signed review of *The Life and Letters of Flaubert* in *Pall Mall Gazette*.

December. Published 'Style', signed, in *Fortnightly Review*; this article draws on the review of Flaubert above.

1889   Pater published seven reviews, some of work by friends, in a variety of journals.

5 April. Published 'Shakespeare's English Kings', signed, in *Scribner's Magazine*.

May. Published 'The Bacchanals of Euripides', signed, in *Macmillan's Magazine*.

August. Published 'Hippolytus Veiled', signed, in *Macmillan's Magazine*.

August. Published 'Giordano Bruno', signed, in *Fortnightly Review*.

15 November. Published *Appreciations: With an Essay on Style*, Macmillan.

Summer. Visited Milan, Bergamo, and Brescia.

1890   March. Second edition of *Imaginary Portraits* issued.

May. Second edition of *Appreciations* issued.

October. Published 'Art Notes in North Italy', signed, in *New Review*.

17 November. Lectured on Mérimée at the Taylor Institution, Oxford, and again (24 November) at London Institution.

23 November. Lectured on Wordsworth at Toynbee Hall, London.

1 December. Elected to Oxford Dante Society.

December. Published 'Prosper Mérimée', signed, in *Fortnightly Review*.

1891   22 January. Pater elected member of Library Committee of Oxford Union; served until 31 March 1892.

July. Attended Speech Day at King's School, Canterbury, where Revd Robert Ottley, an old boy like Pater, an Oxford High Anglican who was Vice-Principal of

(Pusey's and Liddon's) Cuddesdon College 1886–90, and friend of Pater's took the service.

Summer. In Italy, including Florence.

November. Published review of *The Picture of Dorian Gray* by Oscar Wilde (friend) in the *Bookman*.

1892   January. Published 'A Chapter on Plato', signed, in *Macmillan's Magazine*.

February. Published 'The Genius of Plato', signed, in *Contemporary Review*.

May. Published 'Lacedaemon', signed, in *Contemporary Review*.

June–July. Published 'Emerald Uthwart' in two parts, signed, in *New Review*.

August. Third edition of *Marius the Epicurean* issued.

August–September. In France.

September. Published Introduction to Shadwell's translation of *The Purgatory of Dante Alighieri*.

October. Published 'Raphael', signed, in *Fortnightly Review*.

1893   9 February. Published *Plato and Platonism*, Macmillan.

November. Published 'The Age of Athletic Prizemen', signed, in *Contemporary Review*.

November. Published 'Apollo in Picardy', signed, in *Harper's New Monthly Magazine*.

July. With sisters, moved back to Oxford from London.

December. Fourth edition of *The Renaissance* issued.

1894   January. Published 'Some Great Churches in France. 1. Notre-Dame d'Amiens', signed, in *Nineteenth Century*. Pater sat to William Rothenstein for portrait for Rothenstein's proposed book on *Oxford Characters*; in April Pater wrote to the publisher John Lane declining to be included because the drawing displeased his sisters. Nevertheless, the lithograph of Pater appeared in Part VI, in 1895, paired with that of Bussell.

March. Wrote paragraph on Bussell for Rothenstein's book.

April. Received honorary LL D from University of Glasgow.

May. Published 'Some Great Churches in France. 2. Vézelay', signed, in *Nineteenth Century*.

	30 July. Died.
1895	January. *Greek Studies* (Macmillan) appeared, edited by C. L. Shadwell.

February. 'Pascal', signed, appeared in *Contemporary Review*; Edmund Gosse prepared this unfinished piece for publication.

October. *Miscellaneous Studies* (Macmillan) appeared, edited by C. L. Shadwell.

1896   October. *Gaston de Latour* (Macmillan) appeared, edited by C. L. Shadwell. Still unfinished, although periodical form supplemented by new Chapter vi from MS and 'Giordano Bruno' as Chapter vii.

October. *Essays from the 'Guardian'* appeared, privately printed, prepared for the press by Edmund Gosse. Published by the Chiswick Press, which printed the *Century Guild Hobby Horse* for Herbert Horne, and *The Savoy* for Symons and Leonard Smithers.

Abbreviations and References

App.	*Appreciations with an Essay on Style* (Evanston, Ill.: Northwestern University Press, 1987)
BM	*Blackwood's Magazine*
ELT	*English Literature in Transition*
FR	*Fortnightly Review*
GS	*Greek Studies*, ed. C. L. Shadwell (London: Macmillan, 1895)
IP	*Imaginary Portraits* (London: Macmillan, 1887)
Letters	*Letters of Walter Pater*, ed. L. Evans (Oxford: Oxford University Press, 1970)
Marius	*Marius the Epicurean*, ed. I. Small (Oxford: Oxford University Press, 1985)
MM	*Macmillan's Magazine*
PN	*The Pater Newsletter*, ed. H. Ward and L. Brake
Ren.	*The Renaissance: Studies in Art and Poetry*, ed. A. Philips (Oxford: Oxford University Press, 1987)
Studies	*Studies in the History of the Renaissance* (London: Macmillan, 1873)
WM	'Poems by William Morris', *Westminster Review*, 34 (1868), 300–12
WR	*Westminster Review*
Gardner	B. Gardner, *The Lesbian Imagination (Victorian Style): A Psychological and Critical Study of 'Vernon Lee'* (New York and London: Garland, 1987)

Levey   M. Levey, *The Case of Walter Pater* (London: Thames and Hudson, 1978)

Vernon Lee's Letters *Vernon Lee's Letters*, ed. I. Cooper Willis (London: privately printed, 1937)

1

The Subject of 'Pater'

Not the fruit of experience, but experience itself, is the end. A counted number of pulses only is given to us of a variegated, dramatic life. How may we see in them all that is to be seen in them by the finest senses? How shall we pass most swiftly from point to point, and be present always at the focus where the greatest number of vital forces unite in their purest energy?

To burn always with this hard, gem-like flame, to maintain this ecstasy, is success in life.

'Poems by William Morris' (1868), 312; 'Conclusion', *Studies* (1873), 213

These words, which Walter Pater wrote at the outset of his career and reprinted in his first book, dogged him until he died; denounced in the pulpits of Oxford, and celebrated and castigated in the magazines of the 1870s, they reappeared in the obituaries of the 1890s. Much of his subsequent writing was an attempt to explain them, both to the censorious and to his admirers. This implant of defensiveness was not confined to *Marius the Epicurean*, Pater's second book and his only finished novel, which was published *twelve years* after *Studies* in 1885. It affected *Studies* itself: the second edition (1877) excluded the 'Conclusion' entirely; the third (1888) amended and restored it with a nervous explanation which linked it to *Marius*, in which 'the thoughts suggested by it' are 'dealt [with] more fully' (*Ren.* (1888), 246). It persisted to affect important late work, theoretical essays such as 'Style' and his last collection of lectures on Plato and Platonism. Pater's writing career and his conduct of it might be construed as a trajectory of fight and flight from the cultural and historical 'moment' of 1873–4.

In parallel, its influence on his conduct of his *life* might be read as greater, as Pater purposefully left no diaries, journals, or notebooks, and only the most circumspect, and in the vast majority of cases brief, letters. Those who knew him best declined to write a biography, and the job was left to a trio of strangers who began to

1

publish their versions of his life only a decade after his death. Henry James, who knew Pater, characterized him at the time of his funeral as 'the mask without a face' (letter to E. Gosse, Sept. 1894) and this figure of reserve, mystery, and privacy recurs insistently in other memoirs by Pater's friends and contemporaries.

It is only relatively recently that the construction of Pater's life and art, by himself and critics, has itself been construed in terms of the cultural history of homophobia, the homosocial, and gay discourse. In this re-viewing, Pater's entry into gay discourse, in essays of 1867 ('Winckelmann') and 1868 ('Poems by William Morris'), constitutes, in twentieth-century terms, his 'coming out', and the resultant hostility and enthusiasm express respectively the reception of the homophobic and homosocial reading communities. Of course, Victorian aestheticism – an 'ism' which was identified at the time with the poetry of A. C. Swinburne, D. G. Rossetti, and William Morris, and the prose of Swinburne and Pater – includes other discourses, such as philosophy (moral and aesthetic), Christianity, visual art, fashion, craft, and literature, to which critics addressed themselves as well. What is important here is that the politics of aestheticism has come in the late twentieth century to be openly regarded as *gendered*, and specifically but not exclusively implicated in the cultural history of gay male discourse in general, of homoeroticism, and of classical, especially Greek, studies.

Two key books (Eve Sedgwick's *Between Men* in 1985 and Richard Dellamora's *Masculine Desire* in 1990) have now mapped this terrain, which in the past has been the subject primarily of separate authorial studies, but also of topical works (such as Steven Marcus's *The Other Victorians*) which have promptly been marginalized. Post-war work on the history of sexuality, in particular by feminists and the French critic Michel Foucault, has provided impetus for a rereading of literature and culture which brings into view a spectrum of sexualities which inscribes or inhabits discourse in different periods in different ways. Homosexuality and madness, and the cultures attached to them, are viewed as social, historical, and linguistic constructions, examples of what Foucault calls 'subjugated knowledges', knowledges which are disallowed at specific historical periods, and subjects which are discredited by the dominant discourses of experts. Resultant rereadings of literature argue that the spectrum and dialogue of gender may be found in all texts, not only those by 'other' Victorians: all sexuality is contingent and relational, it is claimed, part of a dynamic continuum which both contests and affirms ghettos of sexual practice and discourse. The cultural meaning attached to the term 'manly', for example, in the second half of the nineteenth century may be addressed to other aspects of male behaviour which approach too closely what that culture defines as 'feminine'. Likewise, the claim to desire by women (in the work of Charlotte Brontë, for example) was viewed as 'coarse', 'hysterical'/insane, and 'unwomanly', in so far as desire, in the dominant discourse, was a male, gendered emotion.

It may be seen from the history of legislation, education, and medicine in the nineteenth century, and attempts all over Europe to establish a term for sexual relations between men, that sexuality was both a primary and a policed preoccupation. In Britain, male homosexuality was criminalized in law late, in 1885, and the term 'homosexual' emerged only in the 1890s, with a plethora of other terms such as 'inversion/inverts', 'urning', and 'Greek' being among the more formal terms in use in writing. Without a dominant name and free of formal criminalization until late in the century, what has now hardened into 'homosexuality' was far more fluid in meaning and practice, a situation which in part stemmed from social coercion. Close male bonding and 'romantic friendships' were normalized, as may be seen in *In Memoriam*, Tennyson's series of lyrics dedicated to the life and memory of his beloved friend Arthur Hallam: it was this poem which resulted in the choice of Tennyson as poet laureate and the agreement of his fiancée finally to marry him, assured by the poem of his religious orthodoxy. At the same time there were readers throughout the century who read Tennyson and more explicit work with smaller circulation (the poems of William Cory, for example, a master at Eton) as a knowing coterie; they wrote for and were served by a small number of magazines and a steady supply of mainstream publications with different levels of available meaning; Pater, along with J. A. Symonds, Swinburne, and Oscar Wilde, may be counted among such coterie readers and writers who read and wrote for both mainstream and smaller publications.

If aestheticism has been gendered, it has also been rethought in terms of how it was produced. Prominently, towards the end of the 'Conclusion' from which I have already quoted, Pater circulates versions of a phrase already coined in France, 'art for

Production

3

Rom 'individual'

art's sake', which has come to characterize not only the substance of aestheticism but the model of creation and reception of high art as acts of individual genius. For Pater these acts are conceived in terms of romantic theory, and based in 'passion':

> Only be sure it is passion – that it does yield you this fruit of a quickened, multiplied consciousness. Of such wisdom the poetic passion, the desire of beauty, the love of art for its own sake has most. For art comes to your proposing frankly to give nothing but the highest quality to your moments as they pass, and simply for those moments' sake. (WM 312; *Studies*, 213)

disinterestedness

This claim of art to disinterestedness, to be free of all moral, religious, and political designs on its audience, and of all elements in the producer and the production process which are extraneous to the formal perfection of art, has been contested by materialist or Marxist critics. They have pursued models of cultural production which contextualize art in the matrix of history, class, and a *process* of 'creation', which extend the notion beyond the 'act' to the form in which it circulates (book, magazine, print); to its (re)production (printing, binding, woodcutting, lithography); and to its distribution (circulating libraries, booksellers, magazine subscription or purchase, galleries). This approach to art has particular force when applied to aestheticism, which puts an extreme case for the invulnerability of art to evaluation in terms other than its own aesthetic criteria. In the case of Pater, the wider category of cultural production reveals a producer of culture who carefully regulates his career, 'places' his work, rehashes his material, and, with the aid of the common nineteenth-century option of anonymity for reviewers, both 'puffs' or reviews favourably the work of his friends and protégés and arranges for them to puff his work in turn. These strains in Pater's work – its aestheticism, its internalization of homophobia, its attempt to forge a gay discourse, and its participation in the business of publishing and journalism – coexist; they are not mutually exclusive, though their contradictions are apparent. Far from being unified, Pater's writings accommodate a cacophony of discourses which forestall or even prohibit closure, much as their most crafted, sinuous sentences contrive to do.

Implicit in the concept of cultural production is a comparison between cultural and industrial 'work' and 'production'; art and high culture are one step nearer the products and labour of ordinary work. Postmodernism, in some ways so inimical to Marxism in its dehistoricizing, has, however, furthered the destabilization of the privileged status of art by doing away with an exclusive focus on high culture, and according 'popular' forms of culture full attention. Thus 'ordinary' Hollywood films, promotion videos, television, popular romance, and comics have begun to appear on the syllabuses of hitherto high culture courses such as literature. This has enabled scholars to prise Pater and his writing from his self-proclaimed association with high culture and to take his hitherto invisible and untheorized *practice* into account: to see him as a journalist as well as a critic, and his work as journalism as well as criticism.

This difference of nomenclature was as symptomatic of a contest and a slippage between ideologies in the nineteenth century as it is today, Matthew Arnold's reinvigoration of the terms 'critic' and 'criticism' in his essay in 1864 'The Function of Criticism' and his book *Essays in Criticism* the following year may be seen as an attempt to insert the 'critic' and 'criticism' firmly into the social formation of 'writing' and 'literature' and to free it from the taint of 'interestedness', popular culture, and the press. These pieces collected from periodicals and newspapers became 'essays' not 'articles', making an invisible (ideological) claim to literary discourse and an alternative kind of circulation which denied the ephemeral. In that period and perhaps still within literary discourse today, 'criticism' was a term which masked the (initial) conditions of publication – in the press to deadlines – and Arnold's attempts in 1864–5 may be regarded as a reiteration of the anxiety with which journalism had been viewed historically by 'writers' such as Dryden; but *Essays in Criticism* also became the platform from which he and others launched their attacks on the 'new journalism' in the 1880s and following. The respectability of 'literature' (then a generic term applicable to all writing) was felt to be threatened by the growth of literacy, the mass readership, affordable daily papers, the consequent emergence of journalism as a livelihood and a profession, and the split of writers into authors and journalists and of writing into 'literature' and journalism. A century later, the dominant meaning of 'literature', although contested by postmodernism, still retains traces of this high-culture association which the splitting off of

5

'journalism' made possible. Contemporary theory has addressed this by advocating the substitution of the term 'writing' for 'literature'. However, despite Arnold's efforts, it might be argued that 'criticism' and 'critic' remain terms which 'function' in both high culture and popular discourse, as in the literary or art or cultural 'critic' *and* the cinema or television 'critic' in the daily, weekly, and monthly press. And, it should be said, these 'critics' often function in both cultural formations – as they did in Arnold's day!

Pater was a critic, journalist, writer of fiction, and university teacher. Born in 1839 just after Victoria's accession to the throne, he exhibited in his work a breadth of interests and talents that characterized men of letters in a period before specialization triumphed. In a twentieth-century framework, his most renowned work falls into diverse categories – literary and cultural theory; art history including painting, sculpture, and architecture; classical studies; and the history and criticism of English and modern European literature. The titles of his books – *Studies in the History of the Renaissance, Appreciations with an Essay on Style*, and *Greek Studies* – indicate this range.

With the exception of Classics, none of these subjects could be studied at degree level in most universities in mid-century: although Oxford, where Pater spent his working life, had in Matthew Arnold a distinguished contemporary poet, critic, and journalist as Professor of Poetry, and in John Ruskin a gifted art critic as Slade Professor of Fine Art, it did not offer other teaching, examinations, or degrees in these subjects. Moreover, literature and journalism were only slowly growing into separate discourses, and, like Pater, many academics wrote as scholars, critics, and journalists, although Pater's forays into fiction distinguished him from most of his fellows. The apparent vagueness of the familiar Victorian phrase 'men of letters' emerges as specific, in its accommodation of this generality of interest and practice, and in ruling out women, to whom higher education and degrees were largely closed until the 1880s. Pater, whose sister Clara participated in the fight for higher education for women in Oxford, registered with disapproval this exclusion of women, noting in 'Style' that the 'scholarly conscience' was 'the male conscience . . . under a system of education which still to so large an extent limits real scholarship to men' (*App.* 8). The other side of this gendered access to academic knowledge and discourse was the maleness of the existing university culture, socially and intellectually. Oxford students and dons were all men until 1879, and, with the exception of the heads of houses, until the early 1870s unmarried. In addition, the great number of academic staff were clerics, and until the abolition of the Test Acts in 1871 all university teachers had to be Anglican. Pater lived in college, with the exception of eighteen months, for over a decade and until he was 30, and from the age of 19 he worked and wrote in a closed and homogeneous community in which male bonding, male discourse, and male readers were normal; this had profound repercussions for his life and writing.

2

A Portrait from Life

Pater was the third child and second son of a family of four children born to Maria Pater and her husband Richard between 1835 and 1841 in London. At this time Pater's father and uncle were practising as 'surgeons' in Stepney, a poor dockland East London suburb where Pater was born on 4 August 1839. William, the eldest, leaving school for office work in 1851, subsequently studied medicine, and ended up working away from the family in an asylum for the insane in Stafford. Pater and the two girls – Hester (b. 1837) and Clara (b. 1841) – were to live together from 1869 for the rest of their lives. None of the children married.

Pater lost his father when he was 2 and his uncle when he was 6; probably in 1845 the extended family – his mother, his aunt, his grandmother, and the children – moved to Enfield, where his grandmother died in 1848. They remained there in a rural setting, just north of London, until, in February 1853, Pater (aged 13) entered the King's School, Canterbury, in Kent, as a day pupil, when they moved to Harbledown near the cathedral town. Just a year later the Paters' mother died, and the young people finished their upbringing under their aunt's care. By the time Pater was 14, death had claimed his father, uncle, grandmother, and mother. We know from nineteenth-century records that the deaths of Pater's father and uncle at 45 in the 1840s were not short of the average life expectancy for their class and area (Levey, 11), but the preoccupation with death evident in Pater's writing, as in that of others such as Dickens or Elizabeth Gaskell, is explicable from the regular experience of death, so common in Victorian families.

Little is known of Pater's education before he entered the King's School: he may have attended the grammar school at Enfield for a short time, but in the main he seems to have been privately tutored; it is certain that he followed the curriculum for boys, a principal component of which was Latin and Greek, subjects which Pater later taught to young men at Oxford. It was the possession of knowledge of Classics which qualified applicants for entrance to most universities, and efficiently excluded most women and working men from access to this level of education. Classics was an area of knowledge in England which functioned as definitive of class and gender; it served as gatekeeper. By way of contrast, while we similarly know nothing positive about the education of Pater's sisters at this period, we think that Clara, who also ended up as a tutor in Classics at the University, did not learn Latin until she taught herself as an adult after she moved to Oxford in 1869.

Although Pater gained a commendation in Latin when he left the King's School, his two school prizes were for Ecclesiastical History, another area of scholarship which was normally male. The significance for Pater's life of these male interpretative communities of Classics and Christianity is profound, but I want to note here the ways in which Pater's education at Canterbury was intensely a religious education. We know that life in the King's School, which abutted on to the precincts of the cathedral, was intimately tied to the cathedral building and the rhythms of the Christian calendar and services. In the wake of the defections of the Anglican priests John Henry Newman and Cardinal Manning to the Roman Catholic Church in 1845 and 1851, post-Tractarian[1] Anglicanism was at once defensive and self-critical; ritualist High Churchman and Christian socialists argued the issues. At the King's School Pater met a local High Church vicar, the Revd Edward Woodall (himself later to convert to Catholicism), through a close friend, Henry Dombrain; his family attended Woodall's St Margaret's Church, recently refurbished in the 'Decorated' Gothic style associated with the Tractarian impulse within Anglicanism. Dombrain was one of Pater's two closest friends in school, the other being John Rainier McQueen, who provided after Pater's death much of the information we have about this period of his life. Together the boys were named the Triumvirate, invoking one of the commonplace parallels in the period between the history of the Roman Empire and that of Victorian Britain, and Pater and McQueen were called 'the Inseparables'. Sharing studies, an enthusiasm for attendance at church services, and country rambles, the three spent their school and recreational time together. According to McQueen, Pater extricated himself from the Christian values and personal loyalties of this group in two stages, first shortly before the boys left for university in 1858, when he angrily declared the Triumvirate dissolved, and finally in 1860, when he broke acrimoniously with McQueen, who was unwilling in 1904 to give specific explanations for either event. From McQueen's subsequent behaviour in 1862, when he wrote to the Bishop of London to prevent Pater's ordination in the Church of England, we may infer that Pater's abandonment of religious orthodoxy and what displaced it figured in the rupture; and in McQueen's reticence to Thomas Wright and in his account to Wright of his one-time closeness to Pater, there is a definite sense of a betrayed relationship and a deep loss. Pater's intellectual, spiritual, and emotional transformation from boy to man seems to be profiled in this gradual break with this group and its values. In 1865 also, to symbolize this transformation, Pater burnt an ample manuscript notebook of schoolboy and student poems from his Christian period.

Pater gained a small scholarship from the King's School for his university education and in October 1858 he and McQueen entered Oxford – Pater Queen's College and McQueen Balliol. As Pater had finished school, his aunt and his two sisters left the Harbledown house and established themselves initially in Heidelberg, then in Dresden, probably with the intention that Clara and Hester should learn German for future employment as tutors or governesses; *that* was the female counterpart to the Oxford education in store for one of the two boys in the orphaned family. Pater, in his turn, had no 'home' in Britain apart from his Oxford rooms, and he normally spent his vacations either in Germany or with his London cousins. Although the Paters had a small private income from the legacy of their parents, they were not wealthy; this economic insecurity meant not only that the girls were equipped with skills to work, but that Pater's university life as a student could not be materially lavish, and itself had to result in employment.

Pater seems to have been good friends at Queen's with men such as Ingram Bywater who later were, like himself, distinguished members of the University. His tutor, W. W. Capes, was a young Fellow at Queen's whose special interest was ancient history and whose lectures stimulated students to read widely and critically. Capes, who was ordained only after Pater took his degree, held views apparently so 'broad and rational' that his students were 'a little surprised' when he took Orders in 1865.[2] As an undergraduate Pater impressed his tutors, and he was one of those promising students at the University whom Benjamin Jowett at Balliol offered to tutor for a short stint; Pater and his tutors alike were disappointed when in December 1862 he gained a second-class degree in Literae Humaniores. Just as he took his degree, his plan to be ordained in the Church of England was apparently vitiated by McQueen, who wrote to the Bishop of London to alert him to Pater as an unsuitable applicant; and, in late December, his aunt died in Germany, leaving Pater and his sisters without immediate family.

It was incumbent on Pater to get a paid position. With ordination apparently barred, he chose to remain in Oxford, take students to coach, and apply for Fellowships, some notably clerical. He was also writing, as it was at this period, in 1864, that he was elected to one of the University essay societies called 'Old Mortality', to which he read at least one theologically controversial essay on 'Subjective Immortality' (now lost) and another composition 'Diaphaneitè', which was only posthumously published. Based on C. L. Shadwell, one of Pater's private pupils, 'Diaphaneitè' is Pater's earliest extant 'imaginary portrait'. Shadwell, who won a Fellowship at Oriel, was to be a lifelong friend.

After some unsuccessful attempts to gain a Fellowship over a period of two years, Pater was elected, as a probationer, to the first non-clerical Fellowship (in Classics) at Brasenose College in 1865. As a Fellow, he took up residence in college rooms and opted to tutor, and from 1867 to lecture. One of his renowned tutorial students, in 1866, was the poet Gerard Manley Hopkins, and his earliest lectures were on the history of philosophy. Soon after Pater took up his Fellowship, he published the first of three unsigned review articles in the quarterly *Westminster Review*, and launched his career as critic and journalist parallel to that of university teacher. Journalism had been the other option open to him in 1862, graduating as he did at the height of the growth of periodicals which, since 1859–60, had been swelled by the phenomenon of shilling monthlies such as the *Cornhill Magazine* that, carrying serial fiction, had huge sales. Increasing numbers of graduates who did not wish to take orders and a parish, and who could not gain a Fellowship, went to London to work as journalists. Pater avoided the life of a freelance journalist and instead pursued the periodical market for his writing from the safety of a post which offered him 'in-house' room and board, good libraries, a ready-made social and intellectual community, familiar surroundings, and a salary and a position guaranteed for life. In 1868 Pater contemplated a deeper involvement with journalism, by offering to do a quarterly stint for the *Westminster* as the author of their *Belles Lettres* review section (*Letters*, 5), but it seems to have come to nothing. In 1869 he rented a house in Oxford into which he and his sisters moved. They lived here until 1885, when the Paters established themselves in London, only to return to Oxford in 1893 shortly before Pater's death.

Pater's anonymous essays for the 'wicked *Westminster*' in 1866, 1867, and 1868 were controversial and outspoken; in the first he comments adversely on Coleridge's philosophical and theological absolutism, in the second he praises Greek love, and in the third he savours William Morris's sensuous Pre-Raphaelitism and appends his own hedonist conclusion. In 1869 he published the first of a succession of signed essays on Renaissance artists for the *Fortnightly Review*, which allowed him not only signature but also freedom from the review format and from the 'occasion' of recent publications. These *Fortnightly* pieces, with two of the *Westminster* essays and some unpublished writing, he gathered together to constitute his first book in 1873, *Studies in the History of the Renaissance*. These Renaissance 'studies', so apparently distinct from his tutorial and teaching topics, in part benefited from Pater's early and repeated vacations in Germany, his wider travels on the Continent with his sisters, and in 1865 a journey to Italy with Shadwell, to whom the *Renaissance* volume was dedicated.

I shall discuss Pater's writings separately, and his conduct of a complicated publishing life; suffice it to say that from 1866 onwards Pater published articles, books, and reviews steadily, accreting a varied corpus on classical, modern, and contemporary, English and European topics, most of it falling within the boundaries of literature, history, visual arts, and fiction. Here I want to continue with an account of Pater's academic life in Oxford. As a result of the reception of the *Renaissance* volume in 1873 and the discovery soon after, in February 1874, of some 'compromising' letters written by Pater, his career prospects in the University were seen to be limited: he was passed over for the post of Proctor in 1874, and, although he allowed his name to be put forward as a candidate for the Professorship of Poetry in 1877, he withdrew it before the election, no doubt intimidated by a vituperative and homophobic article on 'The Greek Spirit in Modern Literature' by an Oxford clergyman,

Richard Tyrwhitt, which was more specifically aimed at another candidate, J. A. Symonds, who also withdrew. In 1876–7 he was damagingly parodied, along with a number of other more famous figures associated with Oxford, in a serialized novel, *The New Republic*, which appeared in a fashionable monthly magazine, *Belgravia*; its author, W. H. Mallock, had been a Balliol undergraduate when he wrote it. In 1883 Pater resigned his tutorship to allow himself more time to write *Marius*, his novel of explanation of the philosophy of the *Renaissance*; having completed it, he decided to attempt to lead a fuller life, free of the constraints of Oxford, by taking a London house, and normally only occupying his college rooms on weekdays during term. More than one of Pater's contemporaries noted his meticulous participation in a London society round of dinners, salons, and 'at homes' between 1885 and 1893.

It is clear, however, that the relation between this renowned author and his own university was never comfortable; even as late as June 1893 Edmund Gosse alleges that Pater was not invited to the celebration of the Shelley centenary, and the single honour he received in his lifetime from a British university was an honourary LL D from the University of Glasgow in April 1894. Still, Pater did undertake certain responsibilities in university life, including the Curator of the University Galleries in 1885, and in the same year he stood unsuccessfully for the Slade Professorship of Fine Art vacated by Ruskin. From January 1891 to March 1892 he served as a member of the library committee of the Oxford Union, along with student Union members and his friend Frederick York Powell, historian and a co-founder in 1885 of the *English Historical Review*.

By the mid-1880s Pater had a number of good friends, including, in Oxford, Shadwell at Oriel, T. H. Warren at Magdalen, and perhaps Ingram Bywater at Exeter, although by now the two men differed on questions of university politics and reform. Bywater advocated with Mark Pattison a university of professional scholars and researchers while Pater supported the collegiate system of tutors with its emphasis on undergraduate teaching. In the 1890s Pater became close to a young colleague at Brasenose, the Revd F. W. Bussell, who after Pater's death preached the memorial sermon at Brasenose. In London there was Edmund Gosse the critic and T. H. Ward, a former colleague at Brasenose and a neighbour at Oxford until 1881, when he became a London-based journalist on *The Times*. Other friends of the 1860s and 1870s, such as the painter Simeon Solomon and A. C. Swinburne, Pater no longer saw. Some, such as Matthew B. Moorhouse, a chum from Queen's who became a vicar, and Mandell Creighton, an Oxford contemporary who was elected a Fellow of Merton in 1866, left Oxford to take up livings. Creighton, a High Churchman who later became a Professor of Ecclesiastical History at Cambridge and a bishop, was one of the earliest married Fellows at Merton in 1872.

One source of Pater's circle throughout his life was the stream of undergraduates passing through Oxford. William Sharp noted, in a reminiscence, 'how swiftly responsive he [Pater] was to youth as youth'. After 1873 Pater had 'a following' at the University, and his lectures were well attended by a coterie of student aesthetes and would-be authors and critics, among others. In this setting he met Oscar Wilde (in 1877), whose flamboyance and advocacy of Pater did his idol's reputation no good, D. S. MacColl, Arthur Galton, Lionel Johnson, and Richard Le Gallienne. An additional category of young friends were fledgling authors such as Arthur Symons, William Sharp, and George Moore, to whom Pater was disposed to give generous support: he read proof for Symons and wrote reviews of all three; less close than these was Henry James, whom Pater met in the late 1870s.

By 1884 Pater saw a great deal of Marc-André Raffalovich, a wealthy young Frenchman who wrote poetry (and eventually drama and fiction) and had come to London in 1882 when he was 18 to establish a salon! Raffalovich became a lifelong companion to John Gray, the civil servant and decadent poet who, before he became a Roman Catholic priest, was thought to have been Wilde's model for Dorian Gray. Converting to Catholicism himself in 1896, Raffalovich lived much of his mature life as a patron, helping Aubrey Beardsley with money, for example, at the time of his fatal illness, and building a new church for Gray in Edinburgh. Because of the efforts of Pater's family and friends at the time of his death to suppress or destroy personal papers, Pater's relationships with Raffalovich, and probably many other unnamed acquaintances and friends, is documented only by traces – a sighting here, an allusion there, some few letters, and delayed and veiled reminiscences.

It was in London society at the home of George T. Robinson and his daughter Mary Robinson that Pater met George Moore and

William Sharp, and through Mary too that he met, at the Humphry Wards in Oxford in 1881, one of his women friends, the homosocial novelist Violet Paget, who wrote under the pseudonym of Vernon Lee. It is Violet Paget who offers us both a sighting of Pater with Raffalovich in 1884, and testimony that Pater had women as well as men friends. She notes in June 1893 that 'the Paters had people to tea, 24 women and *no man*! Except Pater' (*Vernon Lee's Letters*, 348), and Burdett Gardner, her biographer, suggests that Pater's sisters liaised between him and a London group of women called 'The Souls' who adhered to the notion of Platonic friendship (Gardner, 548). Pater had other lesbian women friends, such as Katharine Bradley and Edith Cooper, the aunt and niece who wrote verse under the pseudonym 'Michael Field'.

In Oxford itself Pater regularly saw his neighbour Mary Arnold Ward, who, using the name Mrs Humphry Ward, published in 1888 the controversial bestseller *Robert Elsmere*, which Pater reviewed on publication; and in the early years of the Pattison marriage, when the lively and intellectual Emilia Frances Strong Pattison was still in Oxford, Pater was part of the circle she created at Lincoln. Another woman acquaintance of Pater's was Charlotte Green, a fellow-founder with his sister Clara of Somerville. Her connections were formidable: she was wife and from 1880 widow of T. H. Green, the great Oxford reformist and liberal, and favourite sister of J. A. Symonds, who from the safety of Switzerland undertook serious work in the defence of homosexuality. Charlotte Green nursed Pater in his final illness in the spring of 1894 when he suffered from rheumatic fever followed by pleurisy; he died of a heart attack on 30 July of that year, and was buried quietly, in the long vacation, in Holywell cemetery at Oxford.

3

Journalism and Literary Form

With the exception of Pater's two novels, his writing was of lecture, article, review, or short-story length. It never took the form of a continuous academic monograph; its form was determined by the parameters of the commercial periodical press in which it usually appeared before being recycled into volumes. These collections of essays selected from periodical publications were a relatively new way of bookmaking which had developed in the wake of the outgrowth of the periodical press at the beginning of the century; Francis Jeffrey was among the first of that generation to collect his *Edinburgh* essays in volumes, and thus break cover from the anonymous conditions of original publication.

Pater's earliest published work appeared in one of the older quarterlies, the *Westminster Review*, which persisted with anonymity, even in 1866 when anonymity was on the decline in magazine journalism. Between 1866 and 1868 Pater's 'Coleridge's Writings', 'Winckelmann', and 'Poems by William Morris' were all included in its pages as unsigned *reviews*, for quarterlies normally consisted of essays framed as 'reviews' which were linked to the book trade and current publication lists. When in 1869 Pater transferred his work to a new monthly periodical, the *Fortnightly Review*, he was able to abandon anonymity and reviewing at once, for one of the platforms of the new *Fortnightly* in 1865 had been the policy of signature. Moreover, although it called itself a review, like the new market of the monthlies it had dispensed with reviews and published free-standing articles; it also quickly adopted the successful pattern of the monthlies' rhythm, abandoning its titular fortnightly publication after eighteen months to join the monthlies on Magazine Day. The politics of the two journals differed as well, with John Chapman's *Westminster* retaining an element of radicalism with its anonymity, while John Morley's *Fortnightly Review* was more stolidly Liberal.

I would argue that Pater's writing for the two journals which was to form the basis of his first book was sensitive to these differences. Throughout his career, Pater's stints on different periodicals resulted in work *expressive* of those periodicals – their politics, the nature of their readership (men, or men and women; religious or free thinkers), and the conditions of authorship (signature or anonymity; length; pay). Pater's volumes of collected essays (such as *Studies* (1873) and *Appreciations* (1889)) then were doubly eclectic, written on a variety of subjects on numerous occasions in short spurts of prose, but also for different periodicals of distinctive character. What united the essays was Pater's careful, polished style and loose overarching topics, such as English Literature in *Appreciations* and an idiosyncratic notion of the Renaissance in 1873. Undoubtedly the most coherent of Pater's collections of essays is *Plato and Platonism* (1893), which originated in a lecture course.

THE *WESTMINSTER REVIEW*

Pater used the anonymous space of the *Westminster* in his first years as a Fellow to position himself intellectually in his writing, 'aloud' but with safety. The three early essays take as their subjects three unrelated authors who had been subjects of current books – Coleridge, a Romantic poet; Johann Winckelmann, an eighteenth-century German classicist; and William Morris, a contemporary poet. None of them touches on the Renaissance or any single unifying topic. It is unknown whether Pater was sent these books for review by the *Westminster* or chose them himself, but their eclecticism seems to be part of the chance conditions of reviewing recent publications. As it is, Pater declares his relativist theology and independence of Christianity in the first, his sympathy for homosocial life and art in the second, and his commitment to contemporary aestheticism and avant-garde poetry in the third. Another element which signified at the time for contemporary readers was the choice of a German author and the knowledge-able treatment of German philosophy in the Coleridge essay: Germany was regarded as the source of the most up-to-date revisionary theology (Ludwig Feuerbach, for example), and German philosophy and letters were themselves at the cutting edge. Anyone reading these essays retrospectively, knowing they were by the same author, could view their philosophical relativism; their commitment to empiricism, the pursuit of beauty, and passion; their sensualizing of the Middle Ages; and the adherence to the model of Greek life as functions of the rejection of an unhistoricized Christianity in favour of a secular 'higher life' and culture. 'Theology', 'Coleridge Writings' avers, 'is a great house, scored all over with hieroglyphics by perished hands' (*WR* 29 (1866), 129).

Literature and the Romantic Tradition

Pater's essay on Coleridge was the first work Pater published. Appearing in the wake of Matthew Arnold's *Essays in Criticism*, in January 1866, it silently draws on that book for terms such as 'disinterestedness', 'criticism', and 'culture', but contests its insistence that the function of criticism and literature is salvationary, serving culture in religion's stead. Pater's *critique* of Coleridge is that he adhered to the absolute in moral and religious questions, thus obstructing his 'artistic' talent. Reviewing, as he is, an anthology of conversations, letters, and recollections of Coleridge, Pater concentrates on the prose, and expresses (albeit anonymously) a manifest rejection of orthodox Christianity: 'Hard and abstract moralities are yielding to a more exact estimate of the subtlety and complexity of our life' (*WR* 29 (1866), 107). Above all, Pater's essay tacitly addresses Arnold's precipitate rejection of the romantic movement as 'premature', implying not as Arnold argued that the Romantics did not think enough, but that Coleridge thought too much, to the detriment of his poetry, which Pater, however, still judges 'permanently' memorable, along with that of Wordsworth, whose work elicits greater praise. To Arnold's defence of classicism, Pater replies by celebrating relativism, romanticism, and the modern spirit, and by exposing the shortcomings and dangers of the absolute, which Pater damagingly associates with the past and anti-modernity.

Opening with an abstract and philosophical introduction, the review goes on to map three chronologies: that of Coleridge's life, and those of his literary and theological ideas – the literary in the *Biographia Literaria*, Coleridge's self-styled narrative of his own aesthetic growth, and in his Shakespeare criticism; the theological, to which Pater allocates the last third of the review, in *Aids to*

Reflection and *The Friend*. That Pater ends with a resounding flourish in which he identifies the modern with the romantic spirit makes explicit his *endorsement* of 'broken memory' and 'intellectual disquiet' as keynotes of modern life, *Angst* not calm. As for Arnold's version of the Greek spirit, it is, in the penultimate sentence, consigned to the status of 'the Sangraal of an endless pilgrimage' (*WR* 29 (1866), 132).

In his third article for the *Westminster*, nearly two years later, Pater returned to the subject of English poetry in a review of work by William Morris, who had recently published two long narrative poems 'The Life and Death of Jason' and 'The Earthly Paradise'. It is the final pages of this review which Pater extracted, entitled 'Conclusion', and appended as the final essay to *Studies* in 1873. The poems of Morris, a 'late' Romantic, offer Pater another opportunity to posit a relationship between modernity and romanticism, and to construct an alternative to Arnold's history of the modern with its alleged roots in classical Greece and Greek. With the authority of ancient Greece, Arnold attempted to withstand the law of the 'Hebraic' while retaining the husk of its ethical function, but Pater in the Morris review relocates the origins of the modern in a far more recent (European medieval) history, which has, in Chaucer and Malory, an English linguistic element. At the same time Pater silently displaces Ruskin's version of an organic guild- and craft-dominated Middle Ages. The poems' Pre-Raphaelite rendition of Gothic, their proto-Freudian fascination with and fear of the *femme fatale*, and their celebration of male chivalric youth and apostasy allow Pater to explore what appears in subsequent work to be a recurring taste for the macabre, bizarre, erotic, and perverse.

The hedonism of the conclusion to 'Poems by William Morris' (and the 1873 'Conclusion') is addressed to the present of Pater and his readers in the late 1860s, which Arnold was to conceptualize in a characteristically Manichaean and constraining manner as *Culture and Anarchy* in the following year; it explicitly arises from Pater's reading of Morris's Pre-Raphaelite poems. The transfer of the truncated conclusion of that article to *Studies* – necessarily truncated as it involved the insertion of nineteenth-century (contemporary) material into a book on the Renaissance – was bold, dangerous, and retrospectively imprudent, comparable in both its compulsiveness and its outcomes to Oscar Wilde's decision in 1895 to appear in court in the second trial. The characterization of the Romantic school at the outset of the Morris piece as marking a transition from 'a lower to a higher degree of passion in literature' (*WR* 34 (1868), 301) is echoed in the 'ecstasy' and admonition of 'Only, be sure it is passion' in the last paragraph – which was included in what later became the 'Conclusion'. Although the transition of this concluding section of the Morris essay is signalled by contrast – the colour and materiality of Morris's poems against 'the sad-coloured world of abstract philosophy' – the heated vocabulary and the unmistakable engagement of this last section are matched by the diction and provocations of the first: 'The Defence of Guenevere' 'is a thing tormented and awry with passion, like the body of Guenevere defending herself from the charge of adultery' and the Arthurian legends are characterized by 'the strange suggestion of a deliberate choice between Christ and a rival love' (*WR* 34 (1868), 301). This is not a poetry which will fulfil the salvationary function Arnold has proposed, and on which his privileging of poetry above all genres depends.

Early in the essay Pater makes a distinction between the world of all poetry 'in which the forms of things are transfigured' and the 'realities of its time', and Morris's poetry is *twice* removed to a 'spectral' world. By insisting on the *separation* of art from life, and bringing to the theory of realism the problematic of representation, Pater is resisting the constraints of 'morality' on art (as many Victorian writers did). While the notion of *'aesthetic* criticism' as such only appears in *Studies* and develops in 'Giorgione', the roots of 'aesthetic criticism' – which retrospectively appear to be advocacy of the uselessness of art – *prospectively* suggest an insistence on freedom from censorship and the location of art in a formalist discourse which has its own history and language. Pater is not denying the social responsibility of art; he is reacting with others to the exaggerated claims of its exclusive responsibility to society at a particular point in history in which the authority of the State and the Church were crumbling.

In the 'Conclusion' part of the Morris piece, the argument pertaining to art is extended to *any* experience which produces 'passion, insight or intellectual excitement. . . . Not the fruit of experience but experience itself is the end' (*WR* 34 (1868), 311). Like Roland Barthes in the 1950s who 'read' a variety of cultural forms as 'texts',[1] Pater locates art as *one* source of pleasure among others, from 'strange flowers and curious odours, or work of the artist's hands, or the face of one's friend' (*WR* 34 (1868), 311), to 'ecstasy and sorrow of love, [and] political or religious enthusiasm' (*WR* 34 (1868), 312). He foregrounds the notion of the individual and the aesthetic as ingredients of cultural health and individual survival in a period of agitation for political reform (the second Reform Act had just been passed), and when utilitarian notions of the good of the majority and measurement by results were in circulation. In this respect Pater's notion of 'aesthetic criticism' which develops from the mid-1860s is comparable to Sleary's circus world in *Hard Times* a decade before. But one of the most alarming provocations to Victorian readers must have been the disavowal of commitment to *any* theory, habit, '*religious* or philosophical idea' 'which requires of us the sacrifice of any part of this experience' (*WR* 34 (1868), 312; emphasis added). This, and the heightened claims for art as a source of 'passion' in the last sentences of the 'Conclusion', identified the anonymous author of the *Westminster* and the Walter Pater of *Studies* as aligned with apostasy in religion, the Morris–Rossetti strain of Pre-Raphaelitism in art and poetry, and Swinburnian dissent in the face of Arnold and Ruskin, the twin gods *in situ* during Pater's early years at Oxford and nation-wide.

One dominant discourse of the Morris essay not noted so far is that of psychology and science. It is in terms of the laws of physics that Pater constructs the lonely isolated individual whose state and prognosis are dire. The profound sadness of the 'Conclusion' is the other side of the ecstasy. The list of sources of passion ending with 'the face of one's friend' continues:

> Not to discriminate every moment some passionate attitude in those about us and in the brilliance of their gifts some tragic dividing of forces on their ways, is on this short day of frost and sun to sleep before evening. With this sense of the splendour of our experience and of its awful brevity, gathering all we are into one desperate effort to see and touch, we shall hardly have time to make theories . . . (*WR* 34 (1868), 312)

Now, given that the Winckelmann and Morris essays appeared anonymously though successively in the *Westminster* in 1867 and 1868, there is no certainty that the original readers of these two articles would connect them. That 'Winckelmann' and the

'Conclusion' appeared in immediate succession in *Studies* with the author *named* goes some way towards understanding the cumulative effect of the collection of essays during Pater's lifetime. Reading retrospectively after his death, with knowledge of 'Diaphaneitè'[2] as well as of 'Winckelmann', helps readers to link this account of human love and the human condition in 'Poems by William Morris' with the gay discourse discernible in 'Diaphaneitè' and explicit in 'Winckelmann'.

Visual Art, Classicism, and Modernity

The most weighty and pyrotechnical of Pater's early journalism, and the centrepiece of Pater's reviewing for the *Westminster*, 'Winckelmann' covers a biography of the continental Hellenist, and a book by him entitled *History of Ancient Art among the Greeks*. At once it shows Pater's knowledge of the classical world, European intellectual history, and German higher criticism. Where Pater's other reviews treat literature – English prose and poetry – 'Winckelmann' signals an interest in the history and aesthetics of European art, and a grasp extending from ancient statuary to medieval, Renaissance, and modern painting. A full thirty pages and the longest of these essays, it covers a prodigious amount, including the groundwork for the subsequent inclusion of this eighteenth-century topic in a work on the Renaissance. If Winckelmann's neo-classicism looks backward to the Renaissance, his 'Hellenism' is also linked, by Goethe (through whom Pater views and legitimizes Winckelmann as subject), to European romanticism. The rogue presence of Winckelmann and the eighteenth century in *Studies* effects a barely visible transition in the deep structure of the book to the 'Conclusion' and 'the modern [nineteenth-century] world'. With its relation to late nineteenth-century romanticism suppressed by its truncation from the Morris review, the 'Conclusion' becomes usable in *Studies* where 'Coleridge's Writings' is not.

Winckelmann, as Pater constructs him from the biographical information at his disposal, possesses characteristics which typify Pater's writing of the 1860s. A single-minded 'intellectual passion' and 'ardour' drive this figure of the romantic artist/critic. Anticipating the Morris essay and the 'Conclusion', Pater portrays Winckelmann as a young teacher who 'multiplied his intellectual force by detaching it from all flaccid interests' (*WR* 31 (1867), 82); beginning with mathematics and law, this process of detachment extends later in life to renunciation of Protestantism for the patronage of the now Catholic court. At a time when conversion to Rome was an everyday threat to Anglicanism, the combination in the artist of self-denial and sin is provocatively endorsed: 'Certainly at the bar of the highest criticism Winckelmann is more than absolved. The insincerity of his religious profession was only one incident of a culture in which the moral instinct, like the religious or political, was lost in the artistic' (*WR* 31 (1867), 85). While Protestantism is admonished for cutting off Germany from art, Catholicism is praised for its alliance with the pagan! Pater does not leave it there; the basis for the charge of moral corruption of the young levelled against *Studies* probably lies in Pater's claim that Winckelmann's 'enthusiasm' for the Hellenic world was temperamental as well as intellectual. This point is developed explicitly through quotations from letters from 'fervid friendships' on topics which include the superiority of male to female beauty. Youth, a period of manhood recurring in Pater's work, becomes a subject, and its implication in Greek art and the hermaphrodite figure is pursued. As in the Morris essay, Pater's prose is in part a result of an empathy of response to texts under review. Anonymity also permits unrestraint. Quotation, like fiction and 'imaginary portraits', later becomes a technique behind which the authorial voice takes cover. But here, as never before or again, Pater makes explicit his participation in gay discourse. The figured, fervent prose of 'Winckelmann' informs the pieces on Morris and Leonardo, the remaining work of the 1860s. The 'otherness' of gay discourse should be counted among the articulations of resistance to Ruskin and Arnold in Pater's writing.

The address to Ruskin and Arnold in *Studies* as a whole is cumulative and palpable from the Preface onwards. Pater's construction of Winckelmann's sensuous classicism is not that of the disembodied, sanitized Hellenism of Arnold's 'sweetness and light' in *Culture and Anarchy* in 1869 (after 'Winckelmann' but before *Studies*), nor is Pater's view of Morris's sensual but 'useless' verse in accord with Arnold's requirement that English poetry carry the burden of discredited religion and offer models of salvation above all; it is for *that* reason, Arnold explained in his 1853 'Preface', that he suppressed his own poem 'Empedocles on Etna'. In his distinction between Hebraism and Hellenism Arnold tries to draw a fine line between the earnest absolutism of biblical discourse and the grace and enlightened rationality of the classic, but the bottom line is that, while the classical style of free play is preferable, both are 'moral'. In requiring art to be 'moral', Arnold and Ruskin are at one. Where they differ is in Ruskin's choice and vision of period – the Christian Middle Ages, his alliance of 'morality' with cultural labour and material production, and his close interest in craft and *groups* of workmen. The nature of the Middle Ages appreciated in the Morris review, its *femmes fatales*, murderous intrigues, and 'perverse' passions, is irredeemably different from Ruskin's 'manly' vision of honest workman/artists, craft guilds, and Christian gothic. As one reads these essays, Pater's debts to Arnold and Ruskin are evident, but implicit in them as well are his resistance and replies.

I have referred to the breadth of Pater's knowledge, and to the degree to which his writings are journalism as well as criticism. Although it is true that these pieces are written under the *conditions* of journalism, the pieces on Coleridge and Winckelmann particularly are not written in a popular style as we understand it today; they are footnoted, lengthy, include quotations in Greek and German, and discuss theology, philosophy, aesthetics in detail. They are close to our notion of an academic style for publication in a specialist journal. When Pater reprints them in volume form, they tend to lose the footnotes, and as he continues to write for the periodicals he produces less encumbered and far more elegant prose. Pater's prose style – his management of the structure of long and complex sentences and his capacity to produce original and memorable phrases – is what made him famous and notorious in his own day, and even in the heavy logical structures of academic philosophy found in his first published piece on Coleridge we have the following:

> Still, all inward life works itself out in a few simple forms, and culture cannot go very far before the religious graces reappear in it in a subtilized intellectual shape. There are aspects of the religious character which have an artistic worth distinct from their religious import. Longing, a chastened temper, spiritual joy, are precious states of mind, not because they are part of man's duty or because God has commanded them, still less because they are means of obtaining a reward, but because like culture itself they are remote, refined, intense, existing only by the triumph of a few over a dead world of routine in which there is no lifting of the soul at all. (*WR* 29 (1866), 126)

This passage of good, rather than 'fine' writing also illustrates Pater's tendency, associated more with the sermon or persuasive journalism than scholarship, to link his subject, *whatever* it is, to the present day and the question of how to live. Although this is apparently a 'review', Pater moves notably beyond the impersonal evaluation one might expect from this genre, and also habitually discusses books which are not under review. In 1855, in an article on 'The First *Edinburgh* Reviewers', Walter Bagehot had called attention to the characteristic 'review-like essay' and the 'essay-like review' which the great quarterlies created, and in this respect Pater is availing himself of a mode of 'review' which his predecessors had pioneered.

In this passage, too, the coexistence of diverse discourses, such as theology, philosophy, and art, which Pater calls 'culture' may be seen. Throughout his work this insistent 'intertextuality' – by which is meant the co-presence and coalescence in the same work of multiple discourses and texts which enact a kind of dialogue among themselves in the new text which they form – is evident. It might even be said that Pater's great subject is the meeting of competing discourses. I have said that Pater wrote fiction and non-fiction, but as early as the 'Winckelmann' essay Pater uses the pattern of biography and the techniques of fictional narrative which attach to it as the common ground of his writing; that is, there is an unmistakable element of fiction and imaginative writing – plot, suspense, drama, figured language, the passage from birth to death, and above all character – in Pater's non-fiction. Similar in its heterogeniety, his novel *Marius* contains long sections of discursive and exegetical prose explicating the philosophy of Roman religions.

THE *FORTNIGHTLY REVIEW*

When Pater began to write for the *Fortnightly* in 1869 he became free to choose his own subjects and, developing the criticism of visual art and art-criticism that had figured in the consideration of Greek sculpture in 'Winckelmann', he published a sequence of four articles on a single topic – writers and artists of the Italian Renaissance. In these *Fortnightly* pieces Pater refined that merger between the imaginary portraiture of 'Diaphaneitè' and the 'historical' portraiture of 'Winckelmann'. It is a genre which echoes in prose the dramatic monologues of Robert Browning (in *Men and Women* in 1855 and *Dramatis Personae* in 1864) about historical Renaissance characters such as Andrea del Sarto. 'Imaginary portraits' – Pater's generic description of 'The Child in the House' published in 1878 and a subsequent series of short stories of the 1880s about imaginary, historically set figures – also seems to invoke the *Imaginary Conversations* in prose published by Walter Savage Landor earlier in the century. All of the Renaissance essays are biographical 'portraits' which function in the narrative as vehicles or subjectivities for exploration of dangerous material. If Arnold and Ruskin signify authors whose writing Pater reacts against, there is in these Renaissance essays an array of figures whose positions Pater either openly adopts or appropriates and a larger number whose positions are surreptitiously purveyed, with Plato, Goethe, Hugo, and Rousseau exemplifying the former group and Swinburne, Baudelaire, Flaubert, and Simeon Solomon the latter. Pater is particularly artful in quoting others without acknowledgement of the source, or indeed, quotation, at all. Taking on the mask of the lives and views of his 'historical' subjects, Pater makes contentious material – such as (Michelangelo's) vehement passions, (Leonardo's) taste for the grotesque, and (Winckelmann's) preference for Greek love – appear in these 'portraits' as descriptive. These topics all reappear as characteristic subjects in other contexts in Pater's later work.

As a subject, the Renaissance was the corrupt antitype of Ruskin's favoured Middle Ages and Arnold's classical Greece, and Pater could not have made a more topical or pointed choice for these essays and, subsequently, for his first book. Pater was not, however, the only contender in a far wider debate at the time about the period the Renaissance covered and its identifying qualities. Volume vii of Michelet's *Histoire de France*, which treats the Renaissance in France, had appeared in 1855. Within two years of the publication of *Studies*, Joseph Burckhardt had published his work in Switzerland (which Pater had probably not read) and J. A. Symonds's *Renaissance in Italy* (which Pater reviewed) had appeared in England. The issues were not only artistic and moral as Ruskin would have it, and theological (the early, *Christian* Renaissance), but matters of historical interpretation.

Of the four *Fortnightly* subjects – Leonardo da Vinci, Sandro

Botticelli, Pico della Mirandula, and Michelangelo – only the first two primarily concerned visual art. Pico was a Platonist commentator, and, although Michelangelo's artwork takes a strong second place in Pater's essay, it is displaced by the essay title which names its subject as Michelangelo's poetry. I mention this because it might appear at this point that Pater is plumping for criticism of the visual arts. But the first edition of the ensuing book emphasized in its title – *Studies in the History of the Renaissance* – that it was a work of history, and the balance of its contents tipped to writing (five essays) rather than visual art (three essays). Retrospectively, the essays on visual art, such as that on Leonardo, seem decidedly 'literary', caught up in the 'story' narrative of artists' lives and in the *writing* of responses to art. Historically, Pater has been shown to rely on traditional as much as up-to-date scholarship; and twentieth-century research has inevitably defined the corpus of these artists, and exposed works attributed to them by Pater as 'inauthentic'. Even in 1873 a sceptical reviewer denied the claim of the book to 'the historical element'; that this was Frances Strong Pattison, a friend, writing in the *Westminster*, only strengthens the charge. Pater himself seems to have readily agreed: all subsequent editions of the book had the title *The Renaissance: Studies in Art and Poetry.* The longevity and undoubted force of these essays have little to do with their accuracy, and everything to do with their writing. *They* are the object of interest to cultural history, not the work of Leonardo da Vinci as such. Although Pater wrote about art and architecture, he never, unlike his contemporaries Ruskin, S. Colvin, F. T. Palgrave, and Swinburne, devoted even one essay to contemporary nineteenth-century visual art. From brief if numerous allusions in his work, especially his essays on architecture, and from his careful delineation of visual artefacts and architecture in his fiction, it is clear that visual art, contemporary and historical, remained a lifelong interest of Pater's, but he is not an art historian, although a sizeable proportion of his work consists of criticism of visual art. His interests were preponderantly aesthetics, history, language, and prosody.

Nevertheless it is Pater's depiction of Leonardo's *Mona Lisa* which has emerged as the single most well-known piece of Pater's writing. This early, first essay for the *Fortnightly* is in its way as reckless and as bold as the three *Westminster* essays which preceded it: it begins very provocatively by pitting Christianity against philosophy; continuing the intensity of the conclusion from the Morris review, and cultivating further its interest in the 'strange' and perverse, the 'notes' on Leonardo also include, as typical in the life of the artist, an account of his 'Greek' mentor-pupil relationship with Salaino, Leonardo's model for a head 'which Love chooses for its own' 'and afterwards his favourite pupil and servant' (*FR* 6 (1869), 503). Pater's evocative and impressionist description of the *Mona Lisa* helped create the portrait as a cultural icon of the 'mysterious woman'. An analogue to the weary and sensual *femmes fatales* of D. G. Rossetti's Pre-Raphaelite paintings and the poetry of Swinburne and Morris, the passage also echoes closely the book by Arsène Houssaye, which, with Vasari, is acknowledged as a source.

Less visible is the imprint of publishing history. In July 1868 Swinburne published the first article in the *Fortnightly* on Renaissance art, and in 1869 and 1870 Pater adopts, as well as Swinburne's subject, the provisionality of Swinburne's title 'Notes on Designs of the Old Masters at Florence' in his 'notes' on Leonardo and 'fragment' on Botticelli; even the visual-art-based 'studies' of the title of the 1873 volume may be viewed as part of this sequence. Stylistically the resemblance between Swinburne's 'impressions' of pictures and Pater's is unmistakable and Swinburne commented on it wryly at the time. It may well be that Pater decided to move to the *Fortnightly because* of Swinburne's contributions, and a kind of dialogue between the two ensued, possibly authorial but perhaps editorial in origin. Pater's Leonardo essay in the November issue was followed on the next page by Swinburne's poem 'Intercession' and three issues later (in February 1870) by 'The Complaint of Monna Lisa'.

Pater's choice of the Renaissance as a period derives in part from his involvement with Classics, and his interest in both the revival of Classics and the clash and merger of traditions in moments of history perceived as 'transitional'. Pater discusses this throughout the essay on 'Pico' (*FR* 10 (1871), 377), whose account of its subject's death, 'lying down to rest in the Dominican habit, yet amid thoughts of the older gods', articulates the dilemma and anticipates Pater's fashioning of the death of Marius, the Epicurean who is buried as a Christian. Paintings by Botticelli typify for Pater just such a moment, when the Christian motif of the Virgin and child becomes secularized, and when the religious subject is superseded by the mythological. Pater's 'fragment' on Botticelli in 1870, following a chapter on the painter in Crowe's and Cavalcassele's *A New History of Painting in Italy* (1864), is short but it is one of the earlier treatments in English, with Ruskin introducing Botticelli into his Slade lectures only in early 1871.

The last of the *Fortnightly* pieces before the publication of the book, on Michelangelo, is full length, and as dense and finished as 'Leonardo' and as provocative as 'Winckelmann'. It serves as a good example of the way much of Pater's prose was poised on the edge of general acceptability, *just about* passable as public and polite, but offering simultaneously the frisson of the hunt for and delight in a sustained subtext of suggestion accessible to coterie readers alive to nuance. It can be as indirect as 'But about the portals of its vast unfinished churches and its dark shrines, half hidden by votive flowers and candles, lie some of the sweetest works of the early Tuscan sculptors, Giovanni da Pisa and Jacopo della Quercia, things as soft[3] as flowers' (*FR* 10 (1871), 562) or as frank as this allusion to sado-masochism: 'What a sense of wrong in those two captive youths who feel the chains like scalding water on their proud and delicate flesh!' (*FR* 10 (1871), 562). Certain sentences suggest that this is a gendered text which constructs its readers as male and warns off respectable Victorian women: 'We know little of his youth, but all tends to make one believe in the vehemence of its passions. Beneath the Platonic calm of the sonnets there is latent a deep delight in carnal form and colour'; these prepare them for 'He who spoke so decisively of the supremacy in the imaginative world of the unveiled human form had not been always a mere Platonic lover' (*FR* 10 (1871), 563).

STUDIES IN THE HISTORY OF THE RENAISSANCE

To create his volume of *Studies* Pater supplemented these four *Fortnightly* essays with 'Winckelmann' from the *Westminster*, thereby stretching the Renaissance as a period into the eighteenth century. In 1872 he wrote three pieces especially for the book which he did not publish elsewhere; this failure to take advantage of a system which gave him the opportunity to trail his work in the periodicals prior to book publication is unique in Pater's career, with the exception of *Marius* which he had tried to place in

Macmillan's and *Plato and Platonism*. Two pieces which treated Renaissance literature in France – a twelfth-century story ('Aucassin and Nicolette') and sixteenth-century poetry by Joachim du Bellay, one of a group called the *Pleiad* – extended the scope of *Studies* from Italy to France, and introduced the notion of the Medieval Renaissance. The third, on the relief sculpture of Luca della Robbia, persevered with Italian Renaissance visual art. To these essays, arranged in historical chronology, Pater appended a newly written Preface and the 'Conclusion' which consisted of the ending of the 1868 *Westminster* article on Morris.

In the Preface Pater effects a famous sleight of hand which invokes Matthew Arnold's notion of classical criticism which is self-effacing, disinterested, objective only to displace it with 'aesthetic criticism' based in the romantic tradition which is subjective and impressionist: ' "To see the object as in itself it really is," has been justly said to be the aim of all true criticism whatever; and in aesthetic criticism the first step towards seeing one's object as it really is to know one's own impression as it really is . . . .' (*Studies*, p.viii). Much of the adverse criticism that the volume attracted stemmed from this Preface and the 'Conclusion', in both of which Pater made explicit links among the theory of aesthetic criticism, the series of historical studies of the past, and how to live in the present. Pater was accused and suspected of an intent to corrupt youth, and in the following extracts aesthetic criticism is shown to be applicable to life as well as art. Codes of personal conduct are recommended beside codes of reading:

> What is this song or picture, this engaging personality presented in life or in a book, to *me*? What effect does it really produce on me? Does it give me pleasure? . . .

> The aesthetic critic, then, regards all the objects with which he has to do, all works of art and the fairer forms of nature and human life, as powers or forces, producing pleasurable sensations, each of a more or less peculiar and unique kind. . . . To him, the picture, the landscape, the engaging personality in life or in a book, La Gioconda, the hills of Carrara, Pico of Mirandula, are valuable for the virtues, as we say in speaking of a herb, a wine, a gem; for the property each has of affecting one with a special, unique impression of pleasure. Education grows in proportion as one's susceptibility to these impressions increases in depth and variety. (*Studies*, p.ix)

The slippage from art to life is unmistakable, and in itself this is not uncommon in Victorian prose, which in all its manifestations bears the imprint of the sermon – a literary form of familiarity and immense popularity in terms of sales figures. What distinguishes Pater's prose from that of his contemporaries is that moral considerations in this early work are rejected along with all other 'abstract' questions as 'metaphysical questions', 'of no interest' to the aesthetic critic, whose base is empirical and material in its adherence to form.

This initial vision of a life of connoisseurship, of an untrammelled search for aesthetic pleasure, *was* liberating; as his youthful adherents understood at the time. Oscar Wilde called *Studies* his 'golden book'. Throughout Pater's work there is an immense and pervasive wistfulness, a consciousness of the imminence of death at one and the same time as beauty is celebrated and aesthetic pleasure is created. This combination of what Pater depicts as the unlimited potential of experience for beauty and pleasure, and the inevitability of death (a yoking which is characteristic of nineteenth-century decadence) gives an edge to the pursuit Pater recommends, irresistible to late readers as well as to Victorians. This supercharged optimism, which posits an adult reader or viewer stripped of socially constructed inhibition and infinitely open to experience, in the teeth of death, is, I think a large part of why *Studies* continues to be read with pleasure and why it is still liberating. Pater has created a book whose 'subjects' are primarily his theories, language, and style, rather than the Renaissance, the lives of the artists, or their work *per se*. The Renaissance subjects are so visibly mediated that they provide a good example of what Michel Foucault calls 'subjugated knowledges'.

4

Greek and English Studies

If the publication of *Studies* provoked controversy, it also elicited admiration, and Pater produced a steady series of signed essays between 1874 and 1880, most of which appeared in the *Fortnightly*. However, Macmillan, now established as Pater's publisher, managed to solicit contributions from its new author to the firm's monthly magazine, and two pieces in this period appeared there: 'Romanticism' (November 1876) was the third essay on English literature Pater published in the years immediately following *Studies*, the other two being on Wordsworth and *Measure for Measure*; and 'The Child in the House' (April 1878) was Pater's first work of fiction to be published and the first of his 'imaginary portraits'. In September 1880 *Macmillan's Magazine*, under George Grove, published an article 'The New Renaissance; or, The Gospel of Intensity', which attacked aestheticism, and by implication Pater's work. It seems unsurprising, therefore, that Pater did not publish with *Macmillan's Magazine* again until October 1885, but between May 1880 and that date Pater published nothing in a national monthly magazine, presumably because he was working on *Marius*. It is also true that, after 1880, Pater gave very little to the *Fortnightly*, although he did return to it for his important piece on 'Style' in 1888.

If the *Westminster Review* was Pater's periodical during the 1860s, and the *Fortnightly* during the 1870s, *Macmillan's* was his principal place of publication in the 1880s. But this shift accompanies a change in the balance of Pater's writing. Four of his five articles there were fictional 'imaginary portraits' and in 1888 the first five chapters of his novel *Gaston de Latour* were serialized in monthly instalments. Pater did more reviews than ever before, and two of these were for *Macmillan's*. However, the only criticism he published there was on another English figure, Thomas Browne, author of *The Anatomy of Melancholy*. The fact is that Pater occupied himself with writing and publishing fiction in the 1880s, and with reviewing; criticism took a back seat. Much of Pater's reviewing was anonymous, and involved mutual 'puffing' between Pater and his friends, a system also known as 'log-rolling'.

Pater reviewed for a variety of journals, one of them being the *Guardian*, the Church of England paper. After Pater's death the question of his religious beliefs in later life was raised in sermons, reminiscences, and obituaries, with several friends claiming that he had intended to take Orders, or become a Roman Catholic; a number testified to his regular attendance at church. There seems little doubt that by the 1880s Pater's earlier virulence about the Church had abated, and in some profound way he was drawn to the ceremony, the architecture, the capacity to 'believe', and the phenomenon of worship attached to Christianity. *Marius* and a number of the 'imaginary portraits', including the autobiographical 'The Child in the House' and 'Emerald Uthwart' all address these matters.

Between 1885 and 1890 Pater published three books! Two were fiction – a novel (*Marius*) and four short stories (*Imaginary Portraits*). The third was a volume of criticism (*Appreciations*), largely on English literature and collected from work written as early as 1866 and as recently as 1888. He also revised *Studies* for new editions which were published in 1877 and 1888. For 1877 he withdrew the 'Conclusion' without comment, added a second early French story to 'Aucassin and Nicolette', added a vignette as frontispiece, and changed the title to reposition the book in the category of Belles Lettres rather than history. In 1888 he restored the 'Conclusion' with an explanation, and added an essay, 'The School of Giorgione', which had appeared in the *Fortnightly* shortly after the 1877 edition had been issued.

'Giorgione' is suffused with theory, and it begins and ends with large chunks of explicitly theoretical material. Following the lead of the Preface to *Studies*, it immediately identifies 'aesthetic criticism' as its project; in other initial and deft strokes it strives to unseat poetry as the model of the arts to which all other forms strive, and proffers music in its stead. Pater is here signalling his dissent from Arnold, by inserting the 'aesthetic' into 'criticism' and denying the supremacy of poetry among the arts. Imaginative prose is only to be identified as its literary rival in 'Style' eleven years later, but here, in comparison with visual art where *pictorial* qualities are deemed crucial, poetry is viewed as logocentric: it has the disadvantage to address 'with words' 'the mere intelligence' and 'to deal . . . with a definite subject or situation' (*FR* 22 (1877), 529). Given that 'All art constantly aspires to the condition of music' (*FR* 22 (1877), 528), the best poetry for 'aesthetic criticism' is lyric, in which 'a certain suppression or vagueness of mere subject' permits the musical suffusion of matter and form.

This reiterated tendency in Paterian discourse to go beyond the specific work or subject to form and structures calls to mind various facets of later structuralist and poststructuralist work. Thus Pater problematizes the subject of 'Giorgione', noting how uncertain attribution is, and treats Giorgione's work as part of *other* subjects, such as the school of Venice, the history of genre painting, and the relation of Giorgione and Titian. The twelve-page essay only introduces Giorgione five pages in, and the last section of four pages renegotiates the subject by absorbing it into a discussion of the Giorgionesque. Moreover, the biographical 'portrait' at the centre of the essay is full of gaps and openly speculative. Here the Artist has been overtaken by the Artist Function in culture and discourse, much as Michel Foucault argues in 'The Death of the Author'.

These successive new editions of *The Renaissance* (in 1877, 1888, and 1893) testify to the tenacity of the reputation of this first book throughout Pater's lifetime, and to the dissemination of this aestheticism of the 1860s and 1870s through the last third of the century; the young poets of the 1890s had been nursed on Pater's 'golden book'.

ENGLISH LITERATURE AND *APPRECIATIONS*

Having finished *Studies*, Pater continued in the 1870s to spread his energies among diverse areas of work: criticism of English literature and a new area, classical studies, are the categories into which most of his work falls, but there is one more essay on Italian Renaissance art (on Giorgione) and the first short fiction, an 'imaginary portrait'.

The essay on Wordsworth (1874) may be seen as part of Pater's continuing interest in Romanticism, first seen in 'Coleridge's Writings' (1866) but also of a piece with 'Poems by William Morris' (1868). If Arnold declared himself a resolute classicist in 1861–2, and judged the English Romantics to have been 'premature' and suffering from a dearth of knowledge in 1864, Pater resists this on the whole in 1866, while endorsing it in part (Wordsworth lacks 'self-knowledge'), only to become more resolute in 'On Wordsworth' in 1874. There he distances himself clearly from Arnold's position: 'The office of the poet is not that of the moralist, and the first aim of Wordsworth's poetry is to give the reader a peculiar kind of pleasure' (*FR* 15 (1874), 463); he goes on to claim for Wordsworth 'an extraordinary wisdom', which goes a little way towards supplying a 'lesson', if not morality. It is significant that Wordsworth's 'lesson', according to Pater, coincides with one of Arnold's key recommendations: 'the supreme importance of contemplation in the conduct of life' (*FR* 15 (1874), 463). Although Pater seldom names Arnold directly, he conducts tacitly a lifelong dialogue with his activist contemporary, who, in 1881, indirectly replied to Pater in his own essay on Wordsworth.

Subtle, memorable, and well-written, Pater's piece was influential and remains of value. Although it was written in the aftermath of the attacks on the first edition of *Studies*, 'On Wordsworth' continues that book's oppositional stance: it commends the poetry for its sensuousness, for its 'passionate sincerity', and for its capacity 'to appreciate passion in the lowly' and in the pastoral. Nor is the religion of Pater's Wordsworth anodyne or orthodox, but 'a religion of nature'. Pater bases Wordsworth firmly in a radical romantic tradition of nineteenth-century European authors such as Shelley, George Sand, and Théophile Gautier, whose work, politics, and person were controversial at the time Pater was writing; as for Wordsworth himself, Pater likens his process of composition to 'divine possession', that romantic alternative in the ancient world to Aristotle's concept of the poet as the conscious maker of the *Poetics*.

The power that Pater claims for this modern poet is the greatness Arnold appropriated for the ancients. This may be seen in the monumental element in Pater's definition of Wordsworth's posture and achievement: 'the meditative poet, sheltering himself from the agitations of the outward world, is in reality only clearing the scene for the exhibition of emotion, and what he values most is the almost elementary expression of elementary feelings' (*FR* 15 (1874), 460). Pater's praise for the poet's 'bold speculative ideas' confirms that his reading of Wordsworth is designed to establish the poet as part of an indigenous and modern tradition on which late Victorian writing may draw, without having to go back, as Arnold implies, to the ancient world. For Pater, Wordsworth's poetry encompasses realism – that criterion of the modern day – and philosophy: 'But it is, nevertheless, the contact of these thoughts, the speculative boldness in them, that constitutes, at least for some minds, the secret attraction of much of his best poetry – the sudden passage from lowly thoughts and places to majestic forms of philosophical imagination, the play of these thoughts over a world so different' (*FR* 15 (1874), 462). Pater uses the conclusion of this essay, which is a protracted discussion of the priority of means or ends in the conduct of life, to mount an implicit defence of his position in the 'Conclusion' to *Studies* as well as to make an explicit endorsement of Wordsworth's posture of 'impassioned contemplation': 'To witness this spectacle with appropriate emotions', Pater reiterates, 'is the aim of all culture; and of these emotions poetry like Wordsworth's is a great feeder and stimulant' (*FR* 15 (1874), 465). Finally, I want to note that 'On Wordsworth' is among the least biographical, and most critical, of Pater's writings on literary subjects; in that respect, it represents a decided break with *Studies*, and may, like the essay on William Morris, owe its rejection of the biographical mode to the contemporaneity of its subject, with biography representing an invasion of privacy. Whatever the explanation, its conformity to our notions of critical discourse, as well as the space it affords Pater for criticism, may contribute to its esteem in the late twentieth century.

Pater proceeded to scrutinize romanticism as a tradition as well as a period in 1876, wrote on Charles Lamb in 1878, reworked the uncollected Coleridge essay for an anthology in 1880, and went on in 1883 to write a second essay for this anthology of English poetry on D. G. Rossetti, another Pre-Raphaelite poet in the romantic tradition. Additionally, he composed a second 'imaginary portrait' called 'An English Poet' in 1878, which he never published in his lifetime; it appeared in 1931. Although Pater wrote three essays on Shakespeare, and reviews of (largely French) fiction, his single greatest interest in English literature as a critic is Romantic poetry.

These six essays on English literature in the romantic tradition – on Wordsworth, Coleridge, Lamb, Morris, Rossetti, and Romanticism – comprise the core of Pater's volume of 'appreciations' which he published in 1889. As his last piece on English romanticism, 'Dante Gabriel Rossetti' is of interest not least because Pater, by 1883, links Rossetti only glancingly (by allusion to Gray, Blake, and Mary Shelley) with English romanticism or culture. The prime and developed referents here are from continental literature, Dante above all, but also a plethora of French writers – the medieval poet François Villon and the nineteenth-century prose writers Stendhal and Mérimée. As in the Wordsworth article, the approach is textual and avoids explicit biography; however, Pater highlights the cult status of Rossetti's poems ('mainly of an esoteric order' for 'a special and limited audience') and their 'strange' and 'grotesque' imagery to hint at the scandalous biographical details of Rossetti's 'feverishness of soul'. That Rossetti buried the manuscripts of his poems in the coffin of Elizabeth Siddal, and dug them up a decade later, is characteristically referred to obliquely if repeatedly by Pater, for his own cult readers: 'a sense of power in love, defying distance, and those barriers which are so much more than physical distance, of unutterable desire penetrating into the world of sleep, however "lead bound"' (*App.* 238). In the face of the pervasive coded language here, it is perhaps a conscious irony that Rossetti's 'gift of transparency in language – the control of a style which did but obediently shift and shape itself to the mental motion' (*App.* 229–30) is foregrounded, along with the material specificity of detail in the poems, a characteristic which is again obliquely associated with the Pre-Raphaelite style of painting. The sordid circumstances of Rossetti's death from addiction to chloral, just a year before the first publication of Pater's essay, is likewise invoked in codified language by the ascription to Rossetti's poetry of 'insanity', akin to Plato's ' "divine" mania' (*App.* 232). While Pater's construction of Rossetti as a subject – 'to him life is a crisis at every moment' (*App.* 235) – recalls in places the 'portraits' of the Romantic artist in 'Winckelmann' and 'Coleridge's Writings', the obliquity of the essay and its style render it less intense and more reserved. The difference is explained not only by early anonymous rashness and mid-career caution, but by the constraints of contemporaneity which leave critics more free to write of the long dead than of the recently dead whose family and friends remain among your readers. At the same time, the occasion to write of the yoking of death with love is clearly welcome; it is a trope pursued in the Greek studies of the 1870s, and in *Marius*, which Pater was writing at the time he conceived his introduction to Rossetti's poems. And death remains a subject which compels Pater's attention to the end.

It is striking that Pater, champion and author of 'imaginative prose', which he regarded as 'the special and opportune art of the modern world' (*FR* 44 (1888), 730), never engaged with the English novel of his day, except in two reviews for friends – of Mrs Humphry Ward's *Robert Elsmere* (1888) and Oscar Wilde's *The Picture of Dorian Gray* (1891). Pater's and Arnold's neglect, as critics, of Dickens, Thackeray, Charlotte Brontë, Gaskell, Eliot, Moore, Gissing, Hardy, and James seems staggering until it is placed in the context of a general critical undervaluation of the English novel, which was regarded by most critics of the period as a species of light literature with low critical status. Arnold was not alone in believing that 'the future of poetry is immense', which he declared as late as 1880 in 'The Study of Poetry', in the face of the quality, popularity, and ubiquity of English fiction. Retrospectively we may view the nineteenth century as *the* great period of the development of the English novel; that was not the consensus in the period, although certain critics such as George Henry Lewes and Geraldine Jewsbury reviewed novels regularly and campaigned in the press for the scope and achievements of the genre.[1]

THE GREEK ESSAYS

In April 1877, in the course of preparing the second edition of *The Renaissance* for the press, Pater proposed a second book to Macmillan, but it was not until October 1878 that he outlined the contents of a volume entitled *'The School of Giorgione' and other Studies*. Apparently echoing the subject of his first book (the Renaissance), and its title ('studies'), Pater planned an eclectic volume of collected essays to include the pieces on Giorgione, Wordsworth, Romanticism, and Lamb; two short essays on Shakespeare, and two long bipartite pieces on the myth of Demeter and the myth of Dionysus. By November, as printing was under way, Pater changed the title to *'Dionysus' and other Studies* and decided, at the end of the month as he read proof, that he was so dissatisfied with his work that he wished to abandon the book. He could not be dissuaded and accordingly the type was broken up. One factor in his decision may have been the vituperative and widely reported debate about aestheticism and criticism at the libel trial of *Whistler* v. *Ruskin* which took place on

25 and 26 November, just before Pater withdrew the book on 30 November. Whistler's 'damages' of a farthing were derisory, and amounted to defeat. Pater was aware that, in addition to Ruskin, W. H. Mallock and Richard Tyrwhitt (whose disapproving article on 'The Greek Spirit in Modern Literature' had appeared in March) might be counted on to fulminate against his new volume. An important factor was its 'Greek' contents. As Pater read proof, of the Greek studies in particular, he may have decided not to risk reprinting them in volume form in this climate.

C. L. Shadwell, Pater's long-time Oxford colleague and friend, who edited a volume of Pater's *Greek Studies* immediately after Pater died, notes in his Preface that the essays fall into two groups, those that deal with Greek mythology and poetry (i.e. Euripidean drama), and those on art history, specifically sculpture and architecture. The nine essays span three decades, with Pater regularly turning to Greek subjects; five date from the 1870s, four from the 1880s, and one from the 1890s. The first essay in the volume pertains to Dionysus, and was selected by Pater as a title essay of the aborted 1878 volume. The choice of Dionysus, presider over the vineyard and the range of excess and enthusiasm it induces, offers Pater a variety of macabre and recondite material such as Pan and his satyrs, but the whole subject of mythology, an area of study in the forefront of development at the time in Oxford, authorizes him to begin startlingly with the proposition that 'religion' must yield to 'religions' when discussing ancient Greece, and to embark on a discussion of *versions* of the cults of Dionysus, with the implication that religions are human and social institutions rather than divinely determined. He does not scruple to link the second birth of Dionysus each spring with the resurrection of Christ. While allocating ample attraction to the joyous god, Pater turns to the 'melancholy' versions of the god which connect him with human sacrifice, cannibalism, and intense suffering. Throughout this essay, with its range of referents from Greek poetry to nineteenth-century painting, there is licence to dwell on the corporeal as well as the spiritual, the sensual, the repugnant, and the violent.

The following essay on the Bacchanals of Euripides (originally *MM* (1889)) pursues Dionysus in a study of how the playwright draws on the available corpus of myth, and most arrestingly what a production, scene by scene, might entail. It is an impressionist and fevered reading, including accounts of hideous violent acts – 'Pentheus was fallen upon, like a wild beast, by the mystic huntress and torn to pieces, his mother being the first to begin "the sacred rites of slaughter"' (GS 76) – cross-dressing, and recherché detail, all of which illustrate the transgressions of the hegemonic culture that the site of 'Greek studies' at the time permitted, as well as Pater's abiding interest in this licentious element of classical life and male academic discourse. In 'The Myth of Demeter and Persephone' Pater implicitly juxtaposes these elements of Greek religion – the '"worship of sorrow"' – with the hygienic version circulated by Matthew Arnold, as

> a misconception, akin to that which underestimates the influence of the romantic spirit generally, in Greek poetry and art; as if Greek art had dealt exclusively with human nature in its sanity, suppressing all motives of strangeness, all the beauty which is born of difficulty, permitting nothing but an Olympian, though perhaps somewhat wearisome calm. (GS 111)

I want to look briefly at Pater's scrutiny of the art of ancient Greece in Shadwell's volume. Like most of his readers, Pater never travelled to Greece, and he was dependent for his knowledge of Greek art on classical literature itself, with its 'descriptions' of artefacts, contemporary illustrations and books, and holdings of museums in Britain, and in Germany, France, and Italy, which he had visited. Pater's emphasis throughout these essays is on the material and sensuous qualities of the art, with, for example, 'the creations of Greek sculpture' viewed as 'elements of a sequence in the material order, as results of a designed and skilful dealing of accomplished fingers with precious forms of matter for the delight of the eyes' (GS 189). Sculpture is seen to be rooted in early craft work, such as the shield of Achilles and the palace of Alcinous as described in Homer, and metal and wood ornaments and objects. These are impressionist essays, evocative of a holistic culture in which various forms of art combine to occupy the eye. This pervasive attempt to establish the decorative and luxurious nature of Greek art may be in part compensation for the fragmentary state of the Greek remains and their inaccessibility to readers as well as a function of aesthetic criticism with its eye for pleasure, both of which are in evidence below:

> And at least the student must always remember that Greek art was

throughout a much richer and warmer thing, at once with more shadows, and more of a dim magnificence in its surroundings, than the illustrations of a classical dictionary might induce him to think. Some of the ancient temples of Greece were as rich in aesthetic curiosities as a famous modern museum. (*GS* 222).

5

Fictions and 'Portraits'

MARIUS THE EPICUREAN

Marius the Epicurean appeared in 1885 as a two-volume novel. The novel tells the story of Marius, a follower of the Cyrenaic philosophy of pleasure, whose intellectual cast of mind is shaped by his successive and intense friendships (pre-eminently with Flavian, a 'brilliant youth' at school, and Cornelius, a young soldier who harbours Christian knowledge and belief) in the Rome of Marcus Aurelius, the Stoic. It is a pagan world whose brutality and dearth of medical knowledge permit Pater to pursue his preoccupation with death, and to dramatize the argument that the failure of the pagan religions to cope with death convincingly and to provide a satisfactory framework for life leaves the way open to Christianity to dispel the melancholy and sadness with faith, charity, and peace. Moreover, the evident interest of the novel in friendship between young men registers a transition between an initial relationship between Marius and Flavian which is terminated by the death of the latter from the plague and a second friendship, informed by Christianity. It ends with Marius' sacrifice of his life for his friend, whose stake in the (Christian) future and in the optimism Christianity offers is dramatized by his projected marriage with Celia, an idealized Christian woman and the only female main character in the novel. The death of Marius the Epicurean is also cleverly gathered into the new wisdom by the device of the error of the strangers among whom he dies, who take him for a believer and administer communion to the grateful but passive dying man. The conclusion of the novel highlights the attraction of the early Church for those who converted to Roman Catholicism in the nineteenth century, and the attention in the novel to the Roman Catholic Church, as well as the best case for the 'new Cyrenaicism', Pater's version of Epicureanism.

Although possessing certain characteristics of imaginative fiction such as a central character, attention to relations among characters, and detailed presentation of setting, the plot and story are frequently obscured (and even lost) by the incidence of other discourses and genres, notably those of philosophy, history, and criticism. The novel was Pater's attempt to take up the subject-matter of the controversial 'Conclusion' to *Studies* which had been 'withdrawn' since the second edition in 1877, and to deal 'more fully' with it, in order to satisfy his critics. It is evident, however, from the novel as a whole, that Pater's position had changed in the dozen or more years since he had written the *Renaissance* essays, and, while parts of the novel pertain to the 'Conclusion', its overall shape expresses a different sensibility. To a reader of *Studies*, with its disavowal of Christianity and absolutes of any character, Pater's claim in *Marius* that 'the highest Platonic dream is lower than any Christian vision' (*Marius*, 173) signals the nature of that new sensibility, while affording Pater infinite scope for the depiction of the pre-Christian at its best. Another distinct change is the nature of the novel's prose, which is more in command of the nuances of structure, diction, and tone, so that sentences which resemble the following sample are the building blocks of the novel:

> And the inside was something not less dainty and fine, full of the archaisms and curious felicities in which that generation delighted, quaint terms and images picked afresh from the early dramatists, the lifelike phrases of some lost poet preserved by an old grammarian, racy morsels of the vernacular, and studied prettinesses: — all alike, mere playthings for the genuine power and natural eloquence of the erudite artist, unsuppressed by his erudition, which however make some people angry, chiefly less well 'got up' people, and especially those who were untidy from indolence. (*Marius*, 22)

In the light of the cancelled volume of 1878, it might be said that in his choice of second-century Rome, a period of transition between pagan and Christian, Pater avoided the danger posed by the subject of Greek culture, commonly associated with homo-social discourse, and complicated by the violent and grotesque elements in his essays in the 1870s on the decadent afterlife of ancient Greece. *Marius* offers Pater many opportunities: it remains within the professional academic sphere of Classics where Pater's knowledge and imagination are most tenaciously lodged; it can avail itself of the commonplace comparison between Victorian

Britain and the Roman Empire (thus facilitating his attempt to explain the code of conduct recommended to the young in *Studies*, for example); it cunningly finds a vehicle for autobiography in the fictional genre of *Bildungsroman*, and allows Pater to introduce a glimpse of historical Christianity and its intellectual and spiritual potential. As the narrator of the novel is visible, and palpably situated in the nineteenth century, the comparison of the two periods in this respect constitutes an important element of the novel, one which is eased by the availability of the parallel between the two empires at this time.

In one of the many memorable phrases in the novel, the nineteenth-century narrator recommends to his youthful contemporaries 'truant reading' (*Marius*, 32), and aspects of the novel could be termed 'truant' to the same degree as elements of *Studies*. A number of passages contain references and combine discourses in such a way that readers alive to aesthetic vocabulary and texts may produce readings of the text not available to general readers. Although ostensibly in the most popular genre of its day, the novel, *Marius* consists of demanding prose and an abstract and philosophical level of argument which the fictional narrative only negligibly leavens. The readership of *Marius* seemed certain to be smaller and more select than that for *Studies*. However, the interest in Pater's 'reply' to his critics, his following, and the appetite of the Victorian public for novels of religious doubt and faith as diverse as John Henry Newman's *Loss and Gain* and Mrs Humphry Ward's *Robert Elsmere* combined to create demand for a second edition within nine months. *Marius the Epicurean* repays its readers with subtly imagined detail of decadent Rome which incorporates skilfully many classical texts of the period in question. Its halting exquisite progress towards the end of the sway of the pagan and the advent of the Christian manages, obstinately and scandalously, to be a muted celebration of both. Pater was not giving away much to his critics!

IMAGINARY PORTRAITS

Having launched himself as a writer of fiction with *Marius*, Pater produced two more works of fiction within four years. *Imaginary Portraits* appeared in 1887 and consisted of four brief 'lives' of young men of different nationalities and periods. Pater published these short stories successively in *Macmillan's Magazine* between 1885 and 1887. Just as the advent of the shilling monthly magazines after 1859 created a market and facilitated rapid growth of serialized fiction, so the monthlies fostered the short story; it was a genre taken up with enthusiasm by the little magazines of the 1890s such as the *Yellow Book*, the *Savoy*, and their protégés in sympathy with the popularity of the genre on the Continent – in France, Russia, and Germany. Pater's 'imaginary portraits' were hybrids, discrete and standing alone in single issues of *Macmillan's*, and part of a series defined by their *narrative type*. Suiting the serial characteristic of the monthly magazine, which keeps its readers through changing and repetitive elements, Pater's series was also sufficiently unified to form a single volume, with the publication in May of both the final story, in the *Magazine* at the beginning of the month, and the volume itself at the end. Here is a clear case of an author using the press to develop and publicize a projected volume.

The stories are variously set in the past, in eighteenth-century Flanders, medieval France, seventeenth-century Holland, and eighteenth-century Germany, and the displacement of the present, of Englishness, and of the autobiographical by fiction, trebly distance them from charges of corrupting the young. The links between these 'portraits', the fictional 'life' of Marius, and the earlier biographies of the historical figures in *Studies* are palpable; in *Studies* the 'real lives' were sketched imaginatively, as characters in narrative; and in the fiction, the imaginary lives are historicized and documented. In both cases these subjects, fictional and real, are comparable to Browning's array of speakers in his dramatic monologues: they stand stolidly between the writer and his audience, substituting their first person 'I' for his; they screen him *from* his audience.

Two of these stories, 'Denys l'Auxerrois' and 'Duke Carl of Rosenmold', explicitly treat the 'return' or outbreak of the classical world in the modern, and the other two, 'A Prince of Court Painters' and 'Sebastian van Storck', explore northern European culture, particularly painting, in the persons of a Flemish artist (Watteau) and a wayward, philosophical Dutch youth. All die young, and death pervades three of the four tales. Women appear mainly as mothers, sisters, and would-be partners who are quietly ignored (as in 'A Prince') or violently spurned (as in 'Sebastian');

while Duke Carl's love for his peasant-girl fianceé is consummated just before their extinction. There are no marriages, and the bachelor status of three of these young men inscribes a tacit misogyny. As in *Marius*, moments of cruelty and violence, directed at others and self, recur: Denys, a possible murderer, is 'torn at last limb from limb' (*MM* 64 (1886), 423; *IP* 87); Sebastian sets out on 'a continual effort at self-effacement' (*MM* 53 (1886), 358; *IP* 128); Duke Carl decides to 'assist at his own obsequies' (*MM* 56 (1887), 25; *IP* 158), and he and his lover are trampled to death; Antony Watteau 'dismisses' both his lover and his acolyte. In these narratives a predisposition for the exquisite is accompanied by insistence on violence, cruelty, and punishment, as in the verse of Swinburne and Rossetti and in some Pre-Raphaelite and 1890s pictures. None of the tales is transparently written in the period's dominant fictional mode of realism; two make use of the provisionality of the diary or journal form, 'Denys' and 'Duke Carl' adopt qualities of the discourse of the legend, and 'Sebastian' is framed repeatedly in terms of Dutch genre pictures. The narratives are all mediated, *impressions* which reveal their partiality, the filters or lenses through which the narrative is conceived and 'told'.

Gaston de Latour, which appeared in five monthly instalments in the *Fortnightly* from June to October 1888, was the beginning of another novel; a sixth part, titled separately 'Giordano Bruno', was published in August 1889. A parallel to *Marius* set in sixteenth-century France, *Gaston* was abandoned unfinished, and after Pater's death a number of subsequent chapters were found in manuscript. Instead, he published *Appreciations* in November 1889, his first book of literary criticism.

6

Digging Deep

'CRITICISM' AND *APPRECIATIONS*

Appreciations is a collection of eleven essays on English literature, two of which date originally from the 1860s, five from the 1870s, and four from the 1880s; they are drawn from a full range of periodicals – the *Westminster*, the *Fortnightly*, *Macmillan's* and *Scribner's Magazine* – as well as T. H. Ward's anthology of English poetry to which Pater contributed two essays introductory to selections from Coleridge and Rossetti. To compile *Appreciations* Pater had to dig deeply and widely in the past, as his most recent work was primarily fiction.

The book houses two theoretical essays placed in parallel at its beginning and end. 'Style', the opening essay, dates from 1888, and 'Romanticism', here renamed 'Postscript' to fulfil its function as the conclusion, from 1876. Both essays address the position of Matthew Arnold – 'Style' by proposing imaginative *prose* as 'the special art of the modern world', not poetry; and 'Postscript' by concentrating on romanticism and not classicism, and by collapsing Arnold's hard and fast distinctions between the two traditions. Moreover, to parallel Arnold's term 'criticism', Pater offers 'appreciations', a word which values constructive readings which are sympathetic to the text, rather than judgements which arise from external criteria. Another provocative element of *Appreciations* (and one which shows Pater's resistance to censorious pressure) is its reprinting of the 1868 review of William Morris's poems which Pater had raided in 1873 for the controversial conclusion to *Studies*. It also appears disguised, generically renamed as 'Aesthetic Poetry', and, although one reviewer (William Sharp) described it as new, the *Spectator* (21 Dec. 1889, 887–8) associated it with degeneracy, 'rhapsodising', and 'affectation'; when the second edition of *Appreciations* was issued six months later, it had been replaced, still the victim of censorship some fifteen years after *Studies*. In this connection the provenance of 'Style' is of interest, as it too shows Pater's use of the publishing system in producing/writing his work: stemming from an anonymous review of Flaubert's correspondence published in an evening newspaper, the *Pall Mall Gazette* in August 1888, it emerged as 'Style' by December 1888 when the expanded review appeared in the *Fortnightly*, and finally reappeared in November 1889 as the flagship essay for *Appreciations*, a book on *English* literature.

'Style' is notable for defending imaginative prose while presiding over a collection in which no essay is devoted to the English novel and avoiding itself any direct address to the current debate about the censorship of the novel by publishers and circulating libraries, a debate initiated by novelist George Moore and taken up by Thomas Hardy. It is my view that the foregrounding in 'Style' of the formal stylistic elements of prose is an indirect reply to those censors of the novel who claimed priority for its moral contents; and when at the end of the essay it is allowed that stylistic considerations take priority in *good* literature, but that the distinction between good and great literature depends on the quality of contents, Pater tacitly denies any reference to the morality of literature *per se*, emphasizing firmly *other* criteria of quality:

> It is on the quality of the matter it informs or controls, its compass, its variety, its alliance to great ends, or the depth of the note of revolt, or the largeness of hope in it, that the greatness of literary art depends, as *The Divine Comedy, Paradise Lost, Les Miserables, The English Bible*, are great art. (*FR* 44 (1888), 743,*App.* 36)

In so far as the censorship debate about the novel involved charges of sexual explicitness and religious apostasy (e.g. is the novelist permitted to treat adultery? dates on Sunday? the divorce law?), it was extremely dangerous territory for Pater and others whose work had been attacked for just such breaches of public morality. In my view, the defence in 'Style' of the importance of language and style in literature and of 'great' subjects is also a denunciation of censorship of the novel. 'Style' is part of current debate, with Arnold, with the novelists, and with the censors.

I have said that *Appreciations* is Pater's book on English literature, but the collection articulates both the cultural siege under which 'English' was positioned at the time and in particular the continual repression of French literature as the non-tolerated other. In the

1880s in Oxford and elsewhere, the introduction of English into the university curriculum, perhaps to degree status, was widely debated in universities and in the press. At its height in 1886 Pater like many of his peers published work on the question. In February he wrote a review of four textbooks on English literature in the *Guardian*, an Anglican weekly. In November a statement on 'English at the Universities' in the *Pall Mall Gazette* showed him to be anxious to protect Classics; while he cautiously welcomed the study of not only English but modern European literature, the basis of his approval is that literary (rather than philological) work in these modern literatures could aid students in their classical studies. It is at best a tepid endorsement, qualified by the complexity of the position from which it is written; Classical Fellow, reader and reviewer of modern European literature, English author. *Appreciations* has none of the conviction or programme concerning English literature that is found in Hippolyte Taine's history, for example, and, in an important historical moment for 'English', it does not address itself to the provision of a cumulative outline of the canon or the scope of English literature.

In its second edition, *Appreciations*, the book on English literature, is invaded by an essay on a French novel, Octave Feuillet's *La Morte*, added to replace 'Aesthetic Poetry'. However, it was clear to a number of reviewers of the first edition that French literature informed the book: *Blackwood's*, a combatively Tory magazine defending the high moral ground, remarks tartly: 'Greek as Mr. Pater is in soul, his models of style are all French. That is, we think a great mistake' (*BM* 147 (Jan 1890), 144). Three reviews note the appropriation from French of the usage of the word 'appreciations' in the title. The model of Flaubert in 'Style' and discussion of Sainte-Beuve, Stendhal, de Staël, Gautier, Hugo, and others in 'Postscript' alert readers to the way in which English is situated in *Appreciations* and in the culture of the 1880s, with European literature yapping at its heels. French literature is the displaced subject which threatens in turn to destabilize the Englishness of the collection. The other point of the *Blackwood's* reviewer, the displacement of Pater's Greek soul, is also apposite in its reminder that *Appreciations* excludes Pater's extant essays on Greek studies; *eight* in number, the last appearing only fourteen weeks before *Appreciations* was issued, by 1889 these were sufficient in themselves for a book, but Pater never collected these pieces. If *Appreciations* was published instead of *Gaston*, the unfinished novel, it also displaced *Greek Studies*, which was the first book to be edited and issued after Pater's death. Then, in January 1895, after his death and before the trials of Oscar Wilde, it was momentarily safe to publish a book on this unsafe subject.

LAST THINGS

In the last five years of his life Pater developed his existing interests, with essays on Raphael and art in north Italy, Plato and Platonism, and the Greek god in the modern world, but there is a notable turn to French culture, with pieces on Prosper Mérimée, writer of fiction, and Blaise Pascal, the seventeenth-century philosopher; and a new series on French church architecture which Pater contributed to the *Nineteenth Century* (whose editor was an architect), in which he had hitherto published only short, occasional work such as reviews and correspondence. Apart from the volume of lectures on *Plato and Platonism* of 1893, these odd essays were collected posthumously in the aptly named *Miscellaneous Studies* (1895).

One of Pater's late pieces, of 1892, is an imaginary portrait 'Emerald Uthwart', which he placed in two parts in yet another periodical, the *New Review*, in which his work had not yet appeared. In *Miscellaneous Studies* it precedes 'Diaphaneitè', that first imaginary portrait of C. L. Shadwell dating from 1864. It follows 'The Child in the House' (1878), a shorter and slighter piece confined to childhood, and together they have been read by critics as a pair of autobiographical imaginary portraits, sharing as they do distinctive elements: unusually set in England, they self-consciously dramatize memory, focus on child development, foreground autobiography and biography, and chime in odd detail with Pater's own experience – Emerald's and Pater's 'birthday time' is August, and Emerald's school and university experience relate to Pater's in Canterbury and Oxford, which Emerald leaves precipitously for war. At this point the convergence between the author's life and that of his character ends, and the story moves into a discourse of male military romance which involves male companionship, heroic crime, violent punishment, submission, a humiliating reprieve, last-minute glory, and a desired death. It is a plot that at many points touches on sexual fantasy, and daringly ends in a macabre episode of incipient necrophilia included as a 'Postscript, from the Diary of a Surgeon'. Pater's appropriation of an 'objective' scientific discourse for otherwise illicit sexual material is part of a long tradition, but his participation in it late in life shows him to be an author who throughout his life took risks in his writing to explore the possibilities of gender, narrative, and language.

Even from within the eclecticism of late-twentieth-century postmodernism, Walter Pater's writing appears notably diverse, comprising the novel, the short story, essays, journalism, and pertaining to history, art history, Classics, and criticism of literature, art, and architecture. Hailed retrospectively, in our own times, as a proto-modernist, a journalist, and a nineteenth-century practitioner of homosocial discourse, Pater has been read (and latterly dismissed) as a Victorian aesthete and stylist for upwards of fifty years. New criticisms construct new subjects, and cultural theory, gender theory, and the attention to language found in structuralism and poststructuralism all mean that 'Pater' has been revived as a subject. Within the academy, the growth of interdisciplinary study and the transformation of 'English' also mean that the breadth of Pater's writing as a whole may be addressed – not only 'essays' such as 'Style' and the 'Conclusion' which fall into the category of 'literary criticism'. In Pater's writings, that late-nineteenth-century juncture of literature, journalism, academic discourses, and gender discourses may be mapped and savoured by the active reader.

Notes

CHAPTER 2. A PORTRAIT FROM LIFE

1. The Tractarian or Oxford Movement takes its names from a series of pamphlets issued by Anglican clergy between 1833 and 1841 under the title *Tracts for the Times*. Inspired by a sermon on 'National Apostasy' preached by John Keble in 1833, the Tracts defended the Church of England as a divine institution with spiritual authority independent of the State, and attempted to re-establish High Church traditions of the seventeenth century. The Oxford-based clergymen John Pusey and John Henry Newman were central to the movement and the publications, but Newman's *Tract 90* in 1841 and his conversion to Roman Catholicism in 1845 left the movement and the Anglican Church divided. Many conversions and much debate ensued in the following decades, and the influence of the *Tracts* was profound and long-lived. See John Henry Newman's dramatic *Apologia pro vita sua* (1864) and G. Faber, *Oxford Apostles*, 2nd edn. (London, 1936).
2. Charles Sankey, quoted in *John Percival: A Memoir of Canon Capes* (Hereford, 1916), 7.

CHAPTER 3. JOURNALISM AND LITERARY FORM

1. In *Mythologies* (1957) and elsewhere Barthes discusses clothes, *haute cuisine*, and wrestling matches as cultural texts and sources of pleasure.
2. 'Diaphaneitè', thought to be based on Pater's private pupil C. L. Shadwell, was written in 1864 but only published in 1895.
3. The sexual nuance here is enhanced in the 1888 edition and after, where 'soft' is replaced by 'winsome'.

CHAPTER 4. GREEK AND ENGLISH STUDIES

1. For an illuminating view of the neglect of fiction, see Monica Fryckstedt's study of the (scanty) reviewing of fiction in the British press in 1866: *On the Brink: English Novels of 1866* (Uppsala, 1989).

Select Bibliography

WORKS BY WALTER PATER

Collected Editions
Edition De Luxe (London: Macmillan, 1900–1).
New Library Edition (London: Macmillan, 1910).

Separate Works
Studies in the History of the Renaissance (London: Macmillan, 1873).
The Renaissance: Studies in Art and Poetry (1877 ff.), ed. A. Philips (Oxford: Oxford University Press, 1987). An annotated edition of the text suitable for student use.
The Renaissance: Studies in Art and Poetry (1877 ff.), ed. D. Hill (Berkeley and Los Angeles: University of California Press, 1980). This reproduces the 1893 text but provides textual variants, and extensive Critical and Explanatory Notes.
Marius the Epicurean (1885), ed. I. Small (Oxford: Oxford University Press, 1985). This is the text of the third 1892 edition. This edition contains a good introduction and full and scholarly notes.
Imaginary Portraits (London: Macmillan, 1887).
Appreciations, With an Essay on Style (London: Macmillan, 1889; Evanston, Ill., 1987). This is a facsimile of the second 1889 edition, and contains 'Feuillet's *La Morte*' instead of 'Aesthetic Poetry'.
Plato and Platonism (London: Macmillan, 1893).
Greek Studies, ed. C. L. Shadwell (London: Macmillan, 1895).
Miscellaneous Studies, ed. C. L. Shadwell (London: Macmillan, 1895).
Gaston de Latour: An Unfinished Romance, ed. C. L. Shadwell (London: Macmillan, 1896).
Essays from the 'Guardian', ed. E. Gosse, (London: Chiswick Press, 1896), privately printed.
Letters of Walter Pater, ed. L. Evans (Oxford: Oxford University Press, 1970). An annotated edition of Pater's letters with a useful

introduction which includes brief biographies of Pater's friends. A number of letters have been found and published in various periodicals since this volume appeared.

Uncollected Essays, ed. T. Mosher (Portland, Maine: Mosher, 1901).

BIBLIOGRAPHY

Court, F. E. (ed.), *Walter Pater: An Annotated Bibliography of Writings about Him* (De Kalb, Ill., Northern Illinois University Press, 1980). This includes a checklist of Pater's work and an annotated bibliography of selected work about him from 1871 to 1973.

Evans, L., 'Walter Pater', in D. J. Delaura (ed.), *Victorian Prose: A Guide to Research* (New York: MLAA, 1973), 321–59.

Wright, S. *A Bibliography of the Writings of Walter H. Pater* (New York and London: Garland, 1975). An indispensable and fully annotated primary bibliography of Pater's published and unpublished writings, with a number of highly informative bibliographical appendices.

The Pater Newsletter, ed. H. Ward (University of West Virginia, Morgantown) and L. Brake (Birkbeck College, London). Published twice annually, *PN* includes an annotated bibliography in every issue, reviews, and news of Pater studies.

BIOGRAPHY

Benson, A. C., *Walter Pater* (London: Macmillan, 1906). Part of a famous series of succinct biographies, the English Men of Letters, this was one of the earliest biographies of Pater. Benson did not know Pater, but he was assisted by Pater's family and friends.

Brake, L., *Subjugated Knowledges* (London: Macmillan, 1991). Contains two essays on early biographies of Pater by Edmund Gosse and A. C. Benson as well as two other pieces on Pater and the periodicals.

Gardner, B., *The Lesbian Imagination (Victorian Style): A Psychological and Critical Study of 'Vernon Lee'* (New York and London: Garland, 1987).

Gunn, P., *Vernon Lee. Violet Paget, 1856–1935* (London: Oxford University Press, 1964).

Inman, B. A., 'Estrangement and Connection: Walter Pater, Benjamin Jowett, and William M. Hardinge', in *Pater in the 1990s* (London and Greensboro, NC ELT Press, 1991), 1–20. L. Brake and I. Small (eds.). A key article on Pater's early life which draws on correspondence of an undergraduate circle to uncover details of the confrontation between Jowett and Pater in the spring of 1874.

Levey, M., *The Case of Walter Pater* (London: Thames and Hudson, 1978).

The most recent full biography in English, by a renowned art historian. Written from a Freudian perspective, it produces a psychological portrait of Pater through a considered reading of his work and experience.

Monsman, G., *Walter Pater* (Boston: Twayne, 1977). A stylish and pithy biography which includes informed criticism of Pater's writings.

Seiler, R., (ed.), *Walter Pater: A Life Remembered* (Calgary, Alberta: University of Calgary, 1987). An anthology of writings about Pater the man by those who knew him. Arranged in chronological relation to Pater's life, these obituaries, memoirs, articles, reminiscences, and letters provide the reader with much of the raw materials of biography. Contains a detailed chronology of Pater's life, and a valuable introductory overview.

Vernon Lee's Letters, ed. I. Cooper Willis (London, privately printed, 1937).

Wright, T. *The Life of Walter Pater*, 2 vols. (London: Everett, 1907). An investigatory life of Pater and a rival to Benson's Life, which was boycotted by Pater's family and some of his inner circle of friends. Although Wright's enthusiasm for disclosure is strident, his 'indefatigable' research illuminated Pater's early life, and introduced aspects of his later life which have yet to be understood.

CRITICAL STUDIES

Bassett, S., 'The Uncanny Critic of Brasenose: Walter Pater and Modernisms', *Victorian Newsletter*, 58 (Fall 1980), 10–14.

Block, E. Jr., 'Walter Pater, Arthur Symons, and W. B. Yeats, and the Fortunes of the Literary Portrait', *Studies in English Literature*, 26 (1986), 759–76.

Brake, L. and Small, I. (eds.), *Pater in the 1990s* (London and Greensboro, NC: ELT Press 1991.). A collection of essays which represents the range of current work on Pater including editing practices, biography, and a range of theoretical approaches.

Clements, P., *Baudelaire and English Literature* (Princeton, NJ: Princeton University Press, 1985). Reveals Pater's pervasive allusion to and quotation from Baudelaire and his later suppression of it all.

Conlon, J., 'Eliot and Pater: Criticism in Transition', *English Literature in Transition*, 25 (1982), 169–77.

Connor, S., 'Myth as Multiplicity in Walter Pater's *Greek Studies* and "Denys L'Auxerrois" ', *Review of English Studies* (1983), 28–42.

DeLaura, D., *Hebrew and Hellene in Victorian England: Newman, Arnold, Pater* (Austin, Tex., and London: University of Texas Press, 1969). An important book in its time and ours, placing Pater in relation to contemporary cultural and religious criticism.

—————— 'The "Wordsworth" of Pater and Arnold', in *Studies of English Literature 1500–1900*, vi (1966), 651–7.

Dellamora, R., *Masculine Desire: The Sexual Politics of Victorian Aestheticism* (Chapel Hill, NY, and London: University of North Carolina, 1990). Includes three chapters specifically on Pater's work, but the book as a whole is central to contemporary Pater studies.

Dodd, P. (ed.), *Walter Pater: An Imaginative Sense of Fact* (London and Totowa: Cass, 1981). A collection of essays by various authors on a range of approaches to Pater, including a forum on a new edition of Pater's collected works and a bibliography of studies on Pater between 1970 and 1980.

Dowling, L., *Language and Decadence in the Victorian Fin de Siècle* (Princeton, N.J: Princeton University Press, 1986). A poststructuralist re-viewing of the period, in which Pater's work arises *passim*. A key text for anyone interested in nineteenth-century aestheticism and decadence.

Eliot, T. S., 'Arnold and Pater' (1930) in *Selected Essays* (London: Faber, 1952), 431–43. An influential essay which masks Eliot's debts to Pater. Should be read in conjunction with John Conlon's *ELT* article, 'Eliot and Pater'.

Fletcher, I., *Walter Pater* (London: Longman for the British Council, 1959). One of the very best overall estimates of the significance of Pater's work.

Inman, B.A., *Walter Pater's Reading: A Bibliography of his Library Borrowings and Literary References, 1858–1873* (New York and London: Garland, 1981).

—————— *Pater and his Reading, 1874–1877* (New York and London: Garland, 1990). These two volumes are of inestimable value to Pater research, combining as they do identification and glossing of Pater's reading (as extrapolated from his library borrowing) and meticulous and detailed explanation of the links between the reading and his allusive writings.

Iser, W., *Walter Pater: The Aesthetic Moment*, trans. D. Wilson (Cambridge: Cambridge University Press, 1987).

Knoepflmacher, U. C., 'Arnold's Fancy and Pater's Imagination', *Victorian Poetry*, 26 (1988), 103–15. A useful scrutiny of the relation of these two contemporary critics to set beside that of T. S. Eliot and David DeLaura.

Langenfeld, R., Eakin, D., Case, M., Housman, G., and Nadel, I. (eds.), 'Essays in *Marius*', *English Literature in Transition*, 27/1, 2 (1984). Two issues of ELT which constitute an anthology of new essays on *Marius the Epicurean*.

Monsman, G., *Pater's Portraits: Mythic Patterns in the Fiction of Walter Pater* (Baltimore: Johns Hopkins Press, 1967).

—————— 'Narrative Design in Pater's "Gaston de Latour"', *Victorian*

Studies, 23 (1980), 347–67.

—— 'Pater's "Child in the House" and the Renovation of the Self', *Texas Studies in Language and Literature*, 26 (1986), 281–95.

—— *Walter Pater's Art of Autobiography* (New Haven, Conn., and London: Yales University Press, 1980). A deconstructionalist reading of Pater's work.

Peters, R., 'The Cult of the Returned Apollo: Walter Pater's *Renaissance* and *Imaginary Portraits*', *Journal of Pre-Raphaelite Studies*, 2 (1981), 53–69.

Ricks, C., 'Pater, Arnold and Misquotation', *Times Literary Supplement* (25 Nov. 1977), 1383–5. An important essay in the history of criticism opposed to aestheticism, it takes issue with Pater for being an impressionist writer rather than a textual scholar.

Sedgwick, E., *Between Men: English Literature and Male Homosocial Desire* (New York: Columbia University Press, 1985). A ground-breaking book which, from the model of feminist analysis, provides a theoretical framework for discussion of homosocial (male–male bonding), homophobic, and homosexual structures in literary discourse from the Renaissance to the nineteenth century. Although Pater does not figure, chapters on erotic triangles, and works by Thackeray, Dickens, and Whitman are pertinent to Pater studies.

Seiler, R., (ed.), *Walter Pater: The Critical Heritage* (London: Routledge, 1980). An anthology of excerpts from criticism of Pater's work as it appeared in his lifetime in the press and some early twentieth-century assessments, much of it from inaccessible sources.

Shuter, W., 'Pater's Reshuffled Text', *Nineteenth-Century Literature* (1989), 500–25. Examines to good effect Pater's pattern of self-quotation and self-allusion in *Plato and Platonism*. An anatomy of Pater's later style and creative process.

Williams, C., 'Pater in the 1880s: Experiments in Genre', *Journal of Pre-Raphaelite Studies*, 4 (1983), 29–51. Discusses *Marius* as an 'encyclopaedia of genres'. Well worth seeking out.

Index